Contents

Introduction

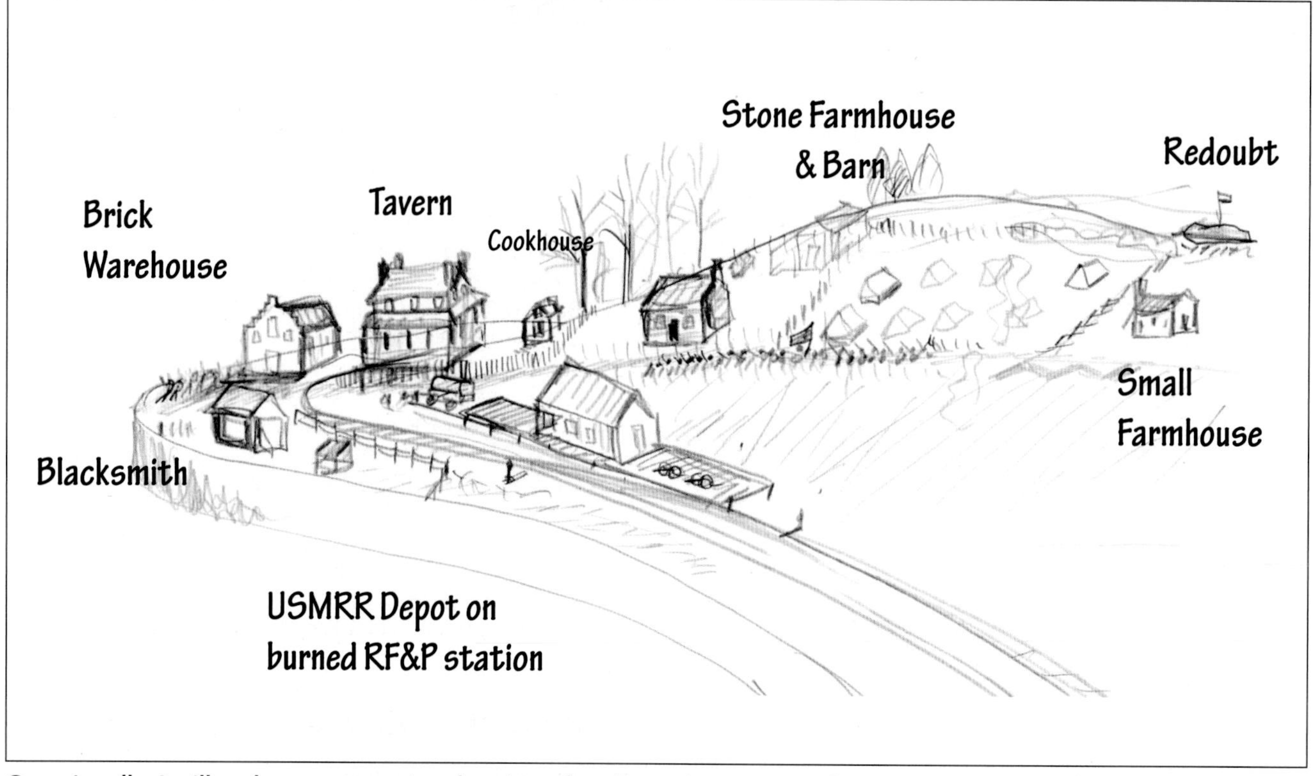

Occasionally, I will make a perspective drawing of a planned scene on a layout to investigate how the elements might look to the viewer. For example, this is a scene planned for my home layout.

I enjoy layout planning. It is my favorite part of this great hobby. This book is a compendium of layout designs that I have developed for my own use or for other people and organizations.

I keep notebooks handy and scribble plans as the ideas come to me. My home office is cluttered with more than a dozen notebooks and sketch pads filled with design ideas. When I haven't had a notebook handy, I have used napkins, scrap paper, pizza boxes, and even a foggy door in the shower to work out ideas for a layout problem that has been vexing me.

Of the thousands of plans I have sketched out, this book features 45 that have reached the final stage of presentation.

Design principles

When designing layouts, I adhere to the following general principles.

Be prototype based. I usually base my layouts on actual prototypes. While I do some freelancing in my designs, they are mostly based on prototype practice.

Keep hidden track to a minimum. In my experience, the hassle of operating hidden track far outweighs any added benefits.

Create a sincere design. *Sincere* is a term coined by model railroaders to describe a layout where the trains run through the scene only once in a session. My layouts try to give a strong sense of going someplace, and a sincere design helps create that feeling.

Maintain a high scenery to track ratio. I try not to cram track into every available square inch of a layout design. I like to give the trains breathing space. This includes simple areas I call "country running" between busy scenes.

Use a walkaround design with aisles that are as wide as possible. The aisles are the easiest part of the layout to build. Make them big.

The layouts

In selecting the layouts for this book, I aimed for a wide variety of subjects, scales, and sizes. They are organized into small, medium, and large designs, and range from shelf layouts to those that can fill a basement or a garage.

There is a slight bias to East Coast railroads because I know them the best, but I have included several from other regions of the United States. Five of the railroads are not in the United States, including one that is set on Mars about 75–100 years from now. Most of these layouts have a theme that tells a story.

I tried to pick subjects that could be built without having to scratchbuild a majority of the rolling stock and/or structures. I also tried to include tips on obtaining specific rolling stock and constructing buildings and scenery.

Some of the smaller layout designs in the book feature a single industry or activity. Most of these plans can be easily expanded into bigger layouts. For example, the Canton Railroad design (pages 6–7) could easily be tacked on to a larger layout as an industry to switch.

Other layout designs are intended for public display at train shows, museums, and other exhibitions. I have been heavily involved in modular model railroads over the past 20 years and have built many modules and portable layouts, as well as some museum displays. I find the interaction with the public while displaying a modular or portable layout to be interesting and satisfying.

Designing a layout for a gymnasium might be a fun theoretical exercise, but almost no one has that much space, except maybe modular clubs at exhibitions, and even they can be limited on space. In all the layouts designed for homes in this book, I used actual layout spaces from places I have either visited or seen in publications. I enjoy designing alternate layouts for these spaces.

Several of the layouts I designed for clients in accordance with their requirements. I find it rewarding to see someone build one of my layout designs. Even if my layout does not get built, it usually aids in the design process of the one that eventually does get built.

These are some of the notebooks in which I have been scribbling layout designs over the years. I like to do the early conceptual work for a layout in pencil on graph paper.

Design software

I frequently get asked about the kind of software I use to draw my final plans. I have tried several drawing packages but I prefer using Adobe Illustrator and Adobe Photoshop.

For most of the design work, I use Illustrator, which is a drawing program with some computer-aided design tools. Photoshop is an industry standard for photo manipulation, but I also use it for advanced graphic work. I use it to add textures and scenery to my drawings. I find a flatbed scanner and a Wacom drawing tablet also useful in doing track plan designs.

I hope you enjoy viewing these plans as much as I did in creating them. Perhaps you will find some ideas useful to your own situation. And if you decide to build one, please drop me a line to let me know how it goes.

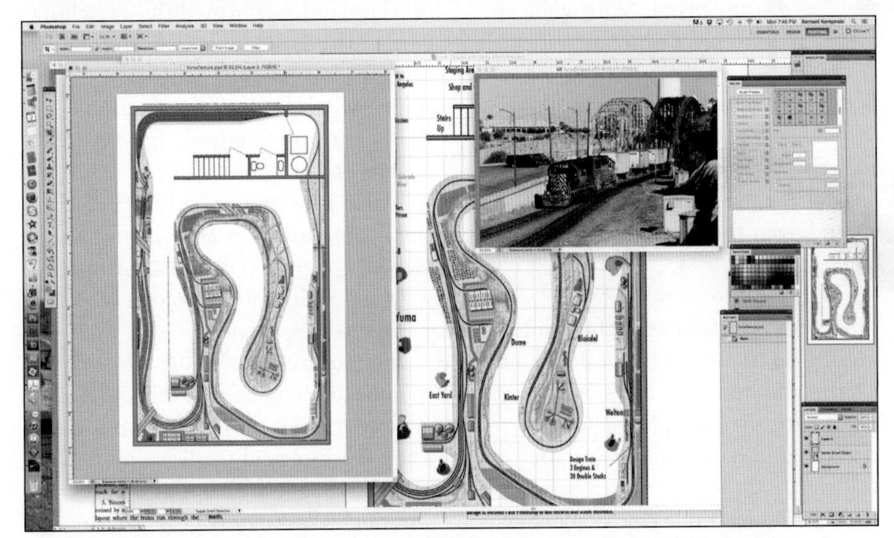

I use Adobe Illustrator for the precise drawing, including the layout of track components, easements, and curve radii. Once the engineering design is finished, I use Photoshop to add textures and scenic elements.

Canton Railroad

Canton 1501, an SW1500, spots a covered hopped at one of the sidings at the Lever Brothers soap factory in Baltimore, Maryland.

Many people starting off in model railroading use a 4x8 sheet of plywood as the base for an oval-shaped layout. This plan cuts the starter 4x8 into two pieces to create a 13-foot-long shape for a realistic point-to-point layout that serves a single large, interesting industry.

The Sun Products (formerly Unilever) soap factory in the Canton area of Baltimore was a local landmark. Occupying nearly 50 acres, it employed several hundred people for seven decades and required one or more trains daily to supply raw materials for making liquid laundry detergent and dish soap. The factory closed in 2014.

The Canton Railroad, a small shortline railroad owned by the state of Maryland, performed the switching duties. The railroad delivered covered hoppers, boxcars, and tank cars. A single switch lead off the Canton Railroad trunk line feeds five separate sidings on the facility.

There is no runaround track, and one is not needed as all the turnouts are facing points. The operators use a scale and weigh house on one of the sidings to weigh cars.

In an operating session, the approaching engine will shove the cars to be spotted to a convenient off-spot. Then the cars ready to leave must be pulled and set aside so that the fresh cars can be spotted. All cars coming and going must be weighed, potentially creating extra switch moves that add operating interest.

With one or two cars, switching is not a great challenge, but as the number of cars increases, the task can be quite daunting.

In the 1990s, the railroad employed various locomotives: an SW1500, a few GP7s, a GP16, and an NW2. Any of these could be used to work the factory. The engines have a distinctive paint scheme based on the Maryland flag.

The factory complex has several main buildings and dozens of small sheds. Complex pipe bridges connect liquid storage tanks. The colorful paint scheme and complex clutter make for fun and challenging models to build.

A temporary staging track can be added under the highway overpass. The layout could also be easily expanded in this direction.

Storage tanks, a scale, and weigh house are located on the north side of the factory. Switching cars to weigh them adds activity to operating sessions.

This photo shows details of the buildings, tanks, railings, and other clutter that add visual interest to the factory. The cylindrical tank on top of the shed is a prominent feature.

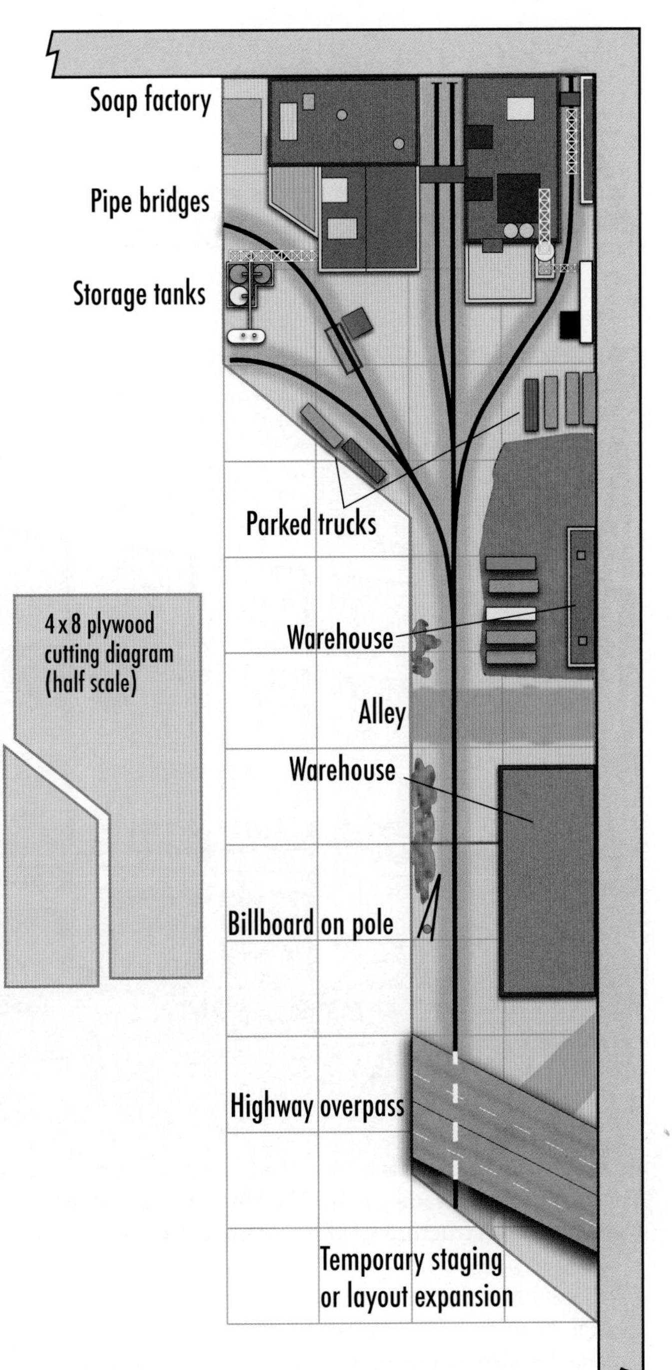

CANTON RAILROAD — HO scale

Size: 4 x 8 feet, expanded to 4 x 13 feet
Prototype: Freelanced
Locale: Baltimore, Maryland
Era: 1990–1999
Style: Shelf
Mainline run: 12 feet
Minimum radius: 22"
Turnouts: No. 6
Maximum grade: 0 percent
Train length: 6–8 cars

Scale of plan: ½" = 1 foot, 12" grid

2

American Can

The distinctive facade of the Machine Services Building with a railroad track running though the corner makes it the signature structure of the complex. The factory was not in service in this early 1990s photograph.

It is not often that you can model an industry in full size without some selective compression. The American Can factory on Boston Street in Baltimore is a interesting manufacturing complex that can be modeled in HO on a 14-foot shelf. In N scale, it requires just under 8 feet.

By the 1990s, the factory was unused. The building was in disrepair, and neighbors wanted it torn down. But it survived. Urban redevelopers renovated it into a shopping mall, offices, and restaurants as part of Baltimore's harbor-side revitalization.

When it was in service, the factory produced tin cans for oyster canning and other industries. In the 19th century, the entire can-making operation was done by hand, including the soldering. By the late 20th century, most of the process became automated. Many of the workers lived nearby and walked to the factory.

The Pennsylvania Railroad (later Conrail) delivered mostly boxcars to the facility. The railroad spotted boxcars containing steel coil at the annex siding, while other boxcars went to the various warehouse sidings. Trucks and trailers also brought in supplies and took out products.

The track plans show the facility in full size with no compression in HO and N scales. The parts of the buildings that do not face the railroad tracks are truncated to fit shelf benchwork. However, the front courtyard and building facades are fully represented.

The N scale track plan shows the complete and accurate track arrangement. There is a little extra room on the right side of the N scale plan to allow switching access to the shipping warehouse sidings.

In the HO version, the plan reverses the sidings into the shipping warehouse, so they can be accessed from the left-hand side. Thus, a switch lead will not be required on the right side of the layout. If the HO layout were integrated into a larger layout, where the main track extends to the right, the

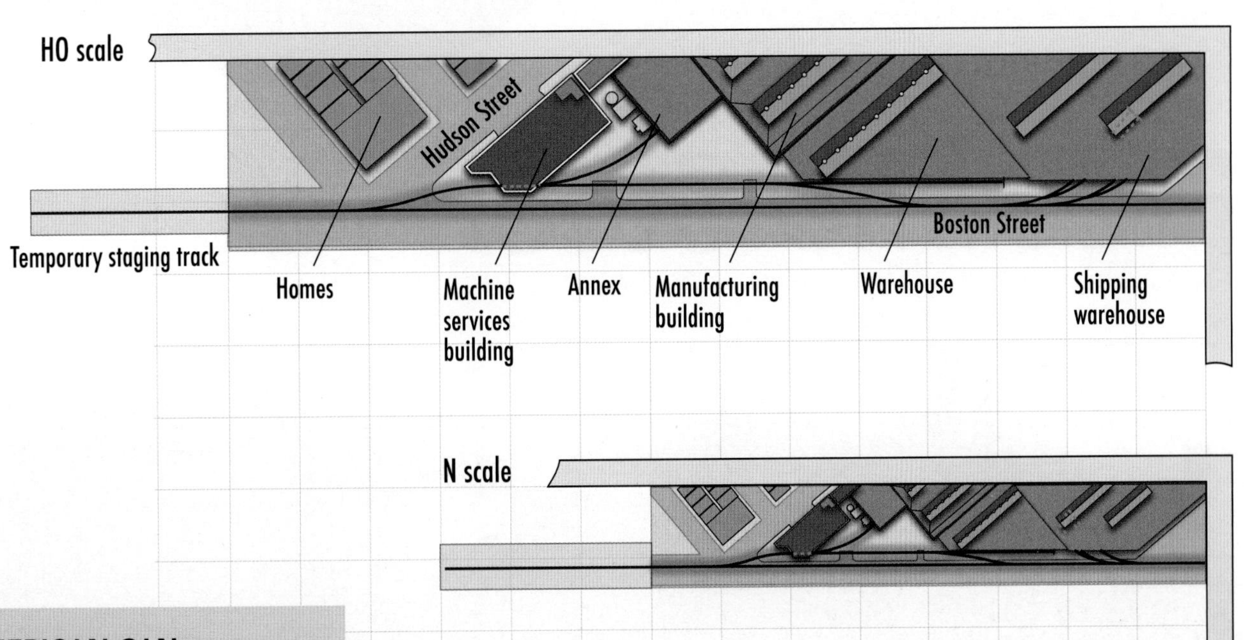

AMERICAN CAN — HO or N scale

Size: HO: 2.5 x 14 feet
N: 1.5 x 8 feet
Prototype: Conrail
Locale: Baltimore, Maryland
Era: 1970–1980
Style: Shelf
Mainline run: HO: 14 feet
N: 8 feet
Minimum radius: 15"
Turnouts: No. 4
Maximum grade: 0 percent
Train length: 3–5 cars

Scale of plan: 3/8" = 1 foot, 12" grid

sidings could be switched back to their correct orientation.

The Machine Services Building is the signature structure. The clipped corner with the track passing through just begs to be modeled. It should be built from scratch to provide an authentic look. I did just that in N scale in 1993 using styrene shapes and screen wire for window sashes.

The brick walls on the warehouses can be simulated with commercially available modular sections. The roofs have several monitor tops with dozens of vents and stacks. Various tanks, fences, and stacks will complete the model and give it a realistic, cluttered look.

The view from the corner of Boston and Hudson Streets shows the track entering the complex passing through the corner of the factory. The courtyard and warehouse facades can be seen in the background at right. *Paul Dolkos*

3

Free-mo Steel

Blast furnace row at Weirton Steel in Weirton, West Virginia, served as inspiration for Free-mo Steel, a layout using Free-mo modules.

Free-mo Steel is a modular layout built to the Free-mo standard. It is loosely based on the Weirton Steel Mill in Weirton, West Virginia.

Free-mo is a modular standard used worldwide. The U.S. Free-mo standard uses a one-track main line. Numerous groups use the standard.

In this design, some adjustments may have to be made to ensure that the through track is in accordance with local users' mainline alignment. (For more information about Free-mo, see free-mo.org.)

This design uses three 3x6 modules to depict the hot end of the steel mill operation. Even with a length of 18 feet, the mill is still very selectively compressed.

The steel mill layout includes the open-hearth furnaces, before the basic oxygen furnace was built, and two blast furnaces.

Because the blast furnace models are based on Walthers kits, they need some customizing of the cast houses to allow the service for hot metal and slag cars, as shown in the plan.

The blast furnace area at Weirton is jammed full of support structures. The design includes some of these, such as the coal gas plant and the loading bridges.

When set up as part of a larger layout, the through tracks run along the center of the modules. As such, it is more suited for a Free-mo branch than a Free-mo mainline module.

Though designed as modules, the modules offer a lot of switching action when set up as a stand-alone layout. They could also be incorporated into a larger home layout if space were available.

The module track plan avoids any turnouts on the module joint. The corners of the framework are notched at the external interface to comply with Free-mo standards.

The 3x6 overall dimensions of each module are probably the largest practical size, as the tall structures add fragile bulk. These module frames should be lightweight but sturdy since the model structures require a stable frame. With a 6-foot frame, the legs can be designed to fold up.

(For more information about Weirton Steel, see my earlier book *The Model Railroader's Guide to Steel Mills*.)

A Conrail train cuts right through the center of the mill, a scene that can be replicated on the layout, as the Free-mo through track runs through the center of the modules.

The gatehouse and the "Extra Quality" sign add interesting detail to a complex industry.

FREE-MO STEEL — HO scale

Size: 3 x 18 feet
Prototype: Freelanced
Locale: West Virginia
Era: 1950–1990
Style: Modular
Mainline run: 18 feet
Minimum radius: 18"
Turnouts: No. 6
Maximum grade: 4 percent on the high line
Train length: 10–16 cars

Scale of plan: ½" = 1 foot, 12" grid

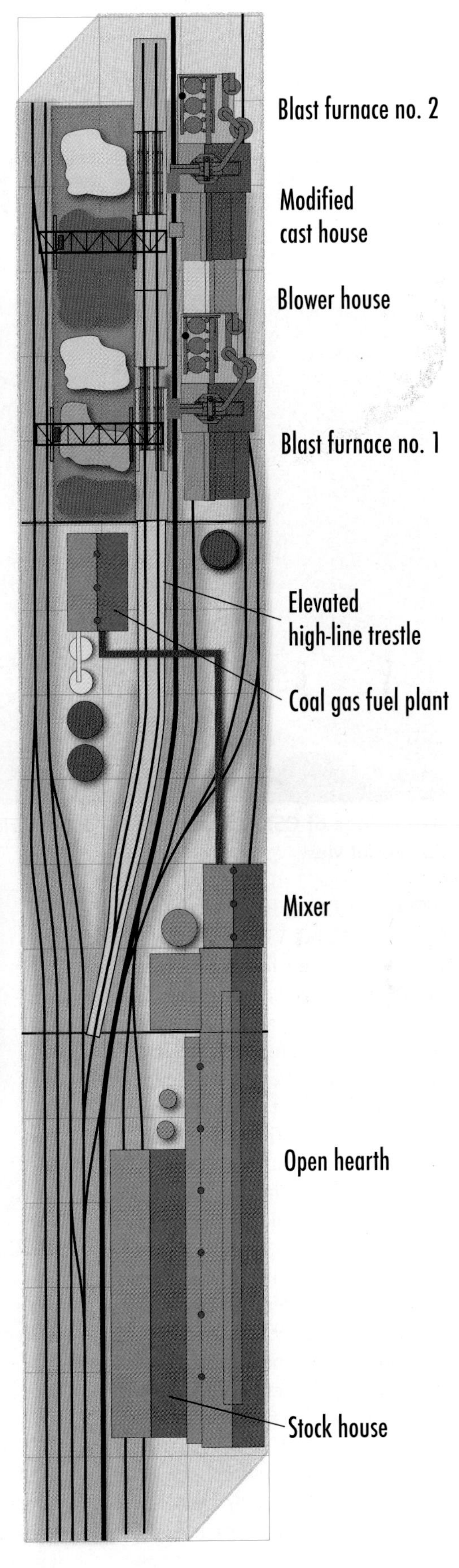

4

Bear Island Paper Mill

Two strings of CSX boxcars can be seen parked on the tracks behind the paper mill and behind the log pile in this aerial view.

The loading crane feeds logs to the debarking machine at left. Once they are stripped of bark, the logs move to a chipper house. The logs are delivered by truck from local forests.

Bear Island Paper Co. in Ashland, Virginia, produced newsprint for use in general printing and newspaper publishing, as well as for advertising circulars. Its customers included newspaper publishers in the United States. Unlike most Southern paper mills, it used a thermo-mechanical process, and not a chemical process, to make pulp. Thus, the mill did not have the extensive chemical processing and by-products facility, typical of other Southern paper mills. It also lacked the distinctive paper mill smell. The mill was built in 1979, and in 2010, the company filed for bankruptcy.

CSX provided rail service from its Piedmont Subdivision just north of Richmond. The paper mill gets boxcars, tank cars, covered hoppers, and coal hoppers. Wood chips come from local logs delivered by truck. You could add a chip and log unloader if you have wood chips and logs delivered to the paper mill by rail. The mill also uses recycled newsprint that is brought in by boxcars.

The track plan is relatively simple and based on the prototype, albeit somewhat selectively compressed. A temporary switch lead (at the upper left of the layout) can help if you wish to simulate trains coming off the main line. Otherwise, you can stage the cars on the siding and use the CSX engine to switch the mill.

For this N scale plan, you can use three hollow-core doors as benchwork. A layer of foam on top of the doors allows for below-grade terrain shaping. This type of construction is useful for apartment dwellers that don't have access to many power tools.

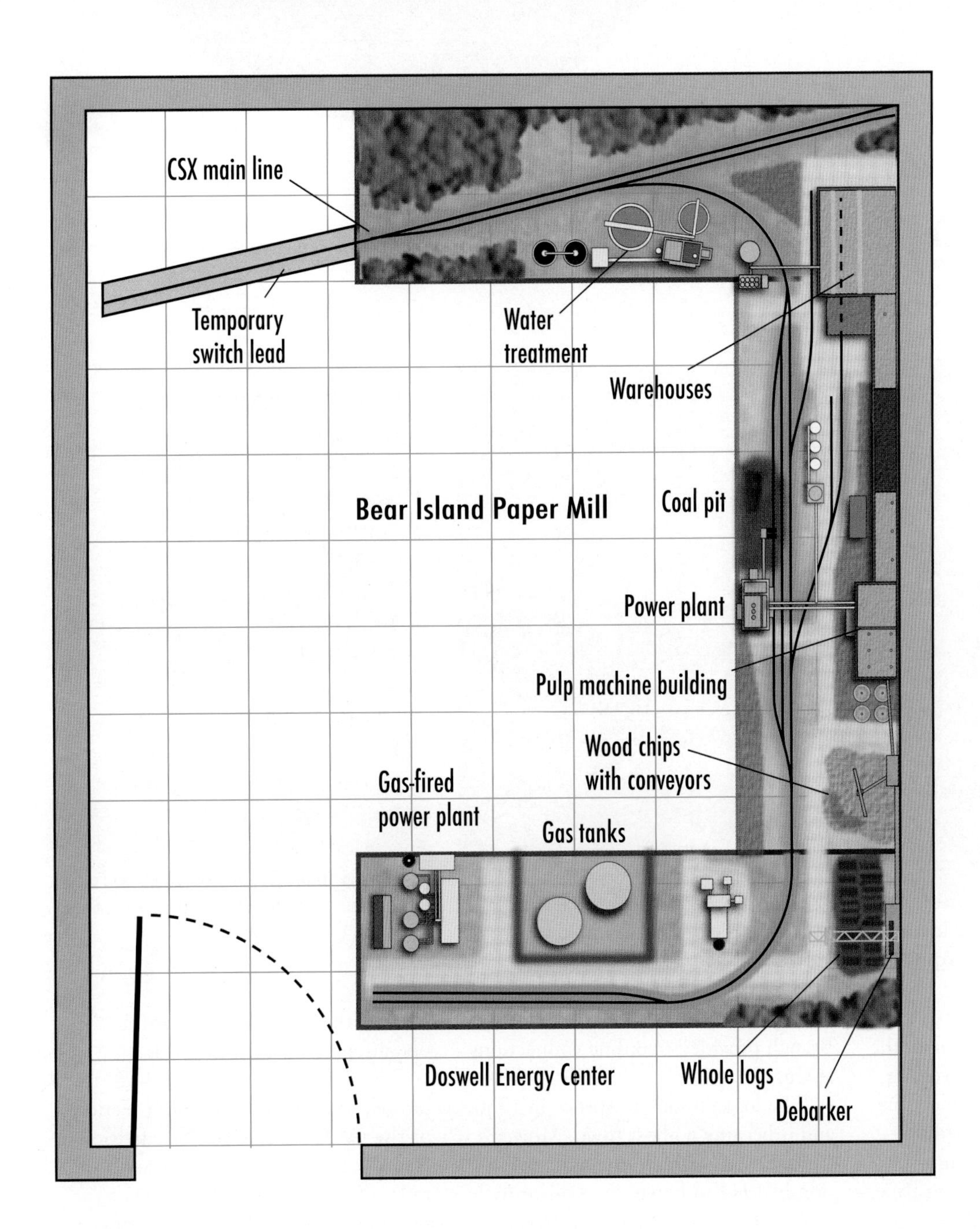

BEAR ISLAND PAPER MILL — N scale

Size: 7 x 11 feet
Prototype: CSX
Locale: Ashland, Virginia
Era: 1997–2010
Style: Shelf
Mainline run: 12 feet
Minimum radius: 18"
Turnouts: No. 6
Maximum grade: 0 percent
Train length: 12 cars

Scale of plan:
½" = 1 foot, 12" grid

Bumpers protect the end of the paper mill storage tracks in front of Doswell Energy Center. The power plant is not rail served as it uses natural gas and steam turbines to generate power 16 hours a day. You could "convert" the facility to oil and attach an oil unloading facility to the power plant to add interest to the layout.

5

Mower Lumber

A Mower Lumber Co. Shay locomotive shoves empty flatcars at a log camp near Spruce, West Virginia. *Paul Dolkos*

MOWER LUMBER — N scale

Size: 8 x 8 feet
Prototype: Mower Lumber Co., C&O, WM
Locale: Cass, West Virginia
Era: 1948–1952
Style: Walk-in
Mainline run: 34 feet
Minimum radius: 12"
Turnouts: No. 6 (and one No. 4)
Maximum grade: 4 percent
Train length: 6–12 cars

Scale of plan: 5/8" = 1 foot, 12" grid

Lumber companies sprouted up throughout West Virginia in the late 19th century to harvest its vast forests. Among railfans, one of the most famous was the Mower Lumber Co. at Cass, West Virginia.

The West Virginian Pulp and Paper mill at Cass predated the Mower Lumber Co. It started in 1900 with 1¼ miles of standard gauge track. The tracks used two switchbacks to gain altitude to the Spruce lumber camp, the highest town in the eastern United States. From Spruce, 250 miles of track radiated in different branches. The mill's 3,000 workers cut and dried 1.5 million board feet of lumber in a week during the peak years of 1908 to 1922. In an average week, 6 to 10 carloads of food and supplies traveled over the railroad to 12 logging camps.

In 1926, the Western Maryland Railway acquired part of the line, while the rest operated under West Virginia Pulp and Paper ownership. The Chesapeake & Ohio Greenbrier Branch provided mainline connections at Cass.

The logs ran out at Spruce in 1930, and it became a ghost town. Mower Lumber Co. acquired the Cass operation in 1942 to harvest second-growth timber. The company re-laid track into old logging areas and set up huge steam skidding machines to bring logs for the mill on the rail lines.

By 1950, the operation was in decline as the secondary growth became depleted. The famous, big four-truck Shays languished on sidings while three overworked and tired three-truck Shays worked the hill. In spite of that, the railroad was very friendly to railfans and would let them ride the trains during operations, with just a signed release.

The rail-haul logging operation and mill ceased operation abruptly on July 1, 1960. In 1961, the railroad was preserved as part of the West Virginia State Park system, and it is still in operation as a tourist railroad.

This N scale plan depicts both the lumber railroad at Cass and a section of the C&O Greenbrier Subdivision. As in the prototype, the lumber railroad tracks climb the hill via a switchback to reach Spruce, now just a lumber camp. Some logs go to the Western Maryland, represented by staging at the back.

The C&O branch is mostly depicted in staging. The C&O trains pick up and drop cars on the interchange tracks in Cass.

The roadbed cutting plan shows how to use one piece of 4x8 plywood to create the roadbed needed for the layout. Conventional open-grid or L girders can be used to finish the rest of the benchwork.

Most of the equipment needed to operate the railroad, including a fine-running two-truck Shay from Atlas, is available in N scale.

4 x 8 sheet roadbed cutting diagram

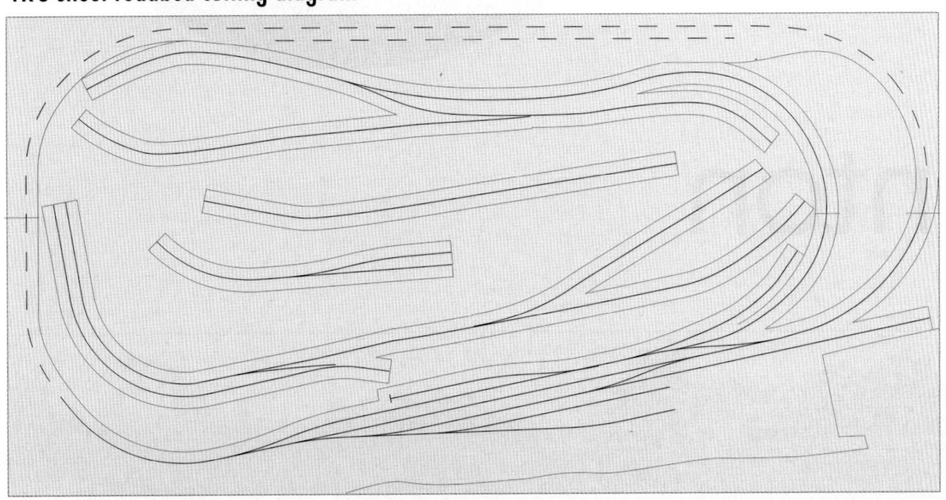

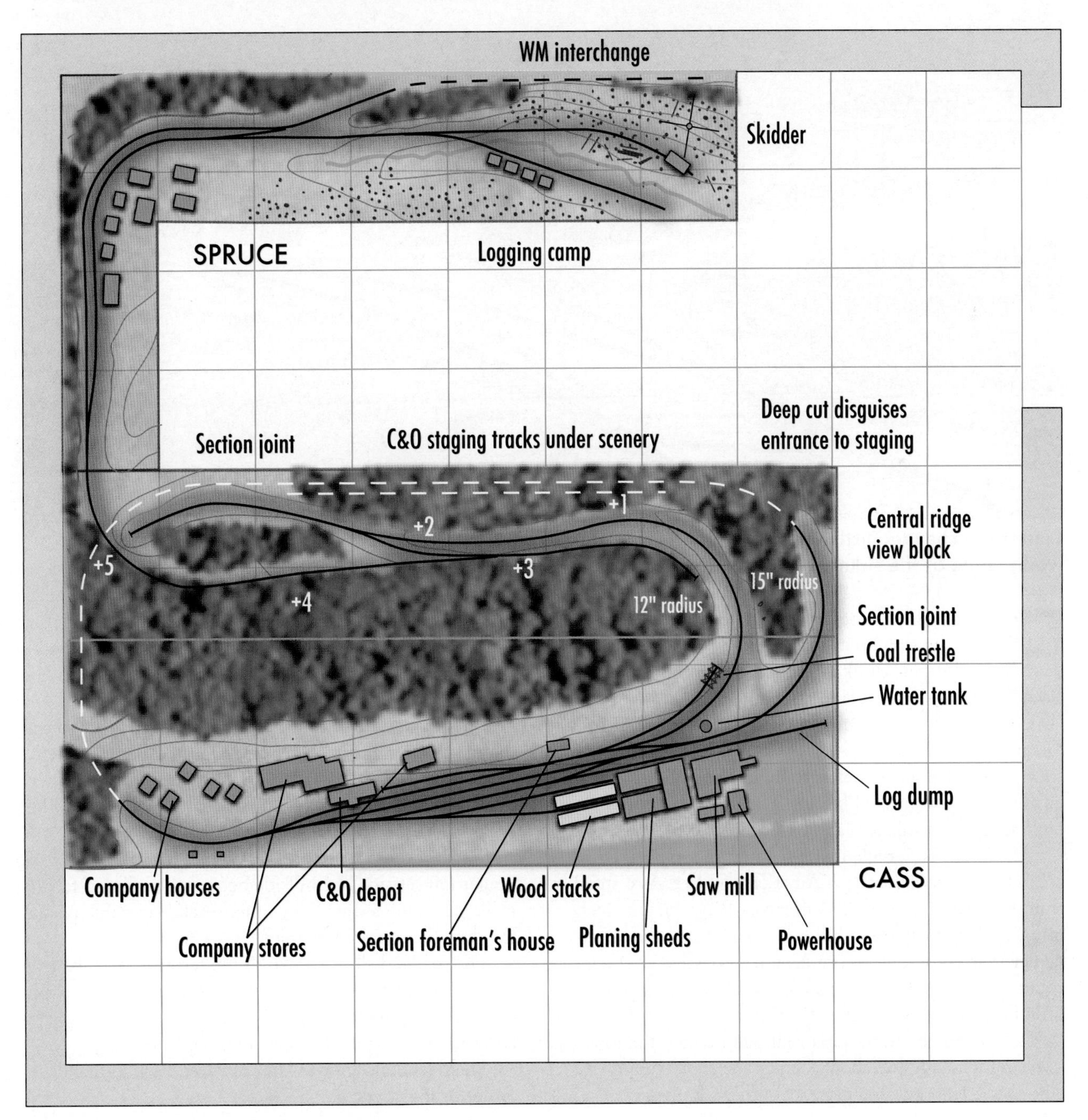

6

Warrenton

Warrenton changed little in the 70 or so years after this photo was taken during the Civil War. Here, a 4-4-0 works some of the sidings. Note the three-way stub switch in the foreground. *Library of Congress*

British railway modelers have a long tradition of building small portable layouts for display at public exhibitions. Unlike most American train shows, display organizers in the United Kingdom pay layout owners to display and operate their model railroads. Generally, the organizers seek the best layouts, so there is strong incentive for modelers to build small but exquisitely detailed and constructed layouts. They frequently include built-in lighting valances and backdrops.

This layout is designed with features of a typical British exhibition layout but with a American subject. As a small stub terminal, the town of Warrenton, Virginia, fits nicely into the British-style exhibition format. While the photos depict Warrenton during the American Civil War, the layout could represent a later period too, as the area changed very little for about 70 years after the war.

The Orange & Alexandria Railroad reached the town via a wye on its main line about 5 miles south of Warrenton. The O&A later became part of Southern Railway.

In town, there was no runaround track, but all the turnouts are facing points. In the Civil War era, a three-way stub switch made for a compact track arrangement. It was later replaced by a set of two regular switches.

The depot had an unusual arrangement with two tracks under awnings and a center track located between two platforms. The photos show 28-foot cars spotted under the eaves. In later eras, two or three 40-foot cars would be spotted at each track.

Some of these structures still stand, though they are no longer rail served. The hillside behind the railroad facility could be simulated with a painted backdrop, some partial building flats, and a few trees.

The roadbed slopes down to the terrain along the front of the layout, creating an excellent location for low-level photos of the rolling stock, while affording good access to work the couplers. The roadbed is now a hiking trail.

The trestle bridge was later replaced with a steel deck girder over a street.

WARRENTON — HO scale

Size: 3 x 6 feet
Prototype: Orange & Alexandria, Southern
Locale: Warrenton, Virginia
Era: 1860–1930
Style: Exhibition
Mainline run: 9 feet
Minimum radius: 36"
Turnouts: No. 6
Maximum grade: 0 percent
Train length: 8 cars

Scale of plan: ¾" = 1 foot, 12" grid

A gentle grassy slope leads up to the tracks and the railroad embankment. The trestle is just out of view on the right side. *Library of Congress*

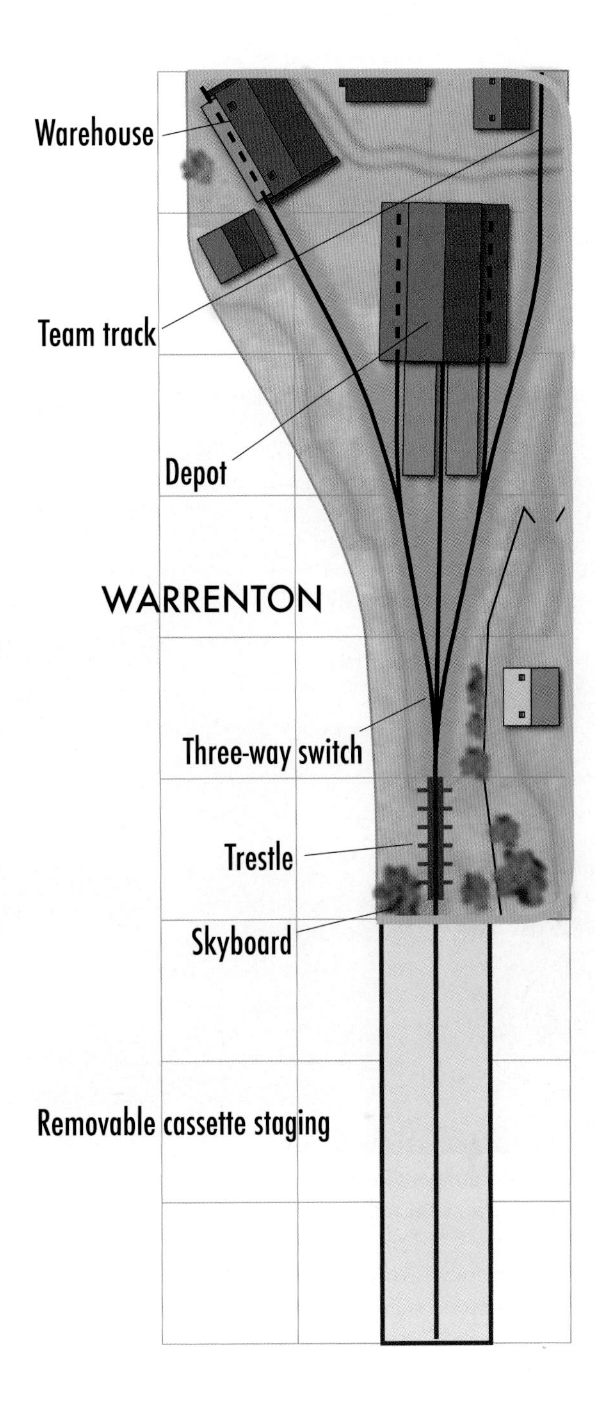

To operate the layout, the conductor/engineer places the desired cars and an engine on the cassette track. The train then shoves the cars onto the layout through a hole in the backdrop. Some strategically placed trees help disguise the hole. Next comes the fun part of figuring out the pulls and spots. The more cars that need to be pulled, the trickier the job becomes.

At 3x6 feet, with an integral valance and skyboard, the layout is bulky, but it should fit in most medium- or larger-sized vans or SUVs. The legs can be built to fold in. With 6 feet of length, the folding legs allow the layout to be placed near eye-level height, making for much more realistic viewing for most adults. Youngsters might need a parent to help them see the layout, but that might not be a bad thing as this also ensures that their little fingers don't touch the highly detailed models that are on display.

The nice thing about a small layout like this is that it can be built in a short time to a high standard. After a few years of exhibiting, it can be sold, retired, or recycled into a new layout.

7

First Steel

Impressive displays like this are part of the fascination of steel mills. Simulating pyrotechnics in scale may be difficult, but a steel mill layout offers many hours of interesting operation and model building. *Siemens GMBH*

Generally a 4x8 sheet of plywood is not a space-efficient configuration for a layout since it usually requires aisles for access from at least three sides, and thereby consumes a big chunk of any room it is in. However, a steel mill railroad is actually a good candidate for a 4x8 design because the width provides plenty of room for the large mill structures. The structures are big enough so they can also serve as a view block across the 4x8 surface, especially if the layout is mounted closer to eye level.

This 4x8 plan is a point-to-point layout that does a reasonable job of simulating the switching at the hot end of a steel mill.

The plan uses many Walthers kits, such as the blast furnace, ore bridge, and rolling mills in nearly stock configuration. There is a small yard at the lower right, where the cars for the mill can be staged, although a temporary extension for staging coming off the lower left would be a worthwhile addition.

The elevated trestle to the high line is an interesting element that enhances the visual appeal of the layout without too much additional complexity. Thanks to the width of the 4x8, there is enough room to show the full width of an open hearth operation including the stockyard for scrap input on the left and the ingot stripping on the right.

Because it is a small layout, the operation is limited to switching many of the specialized steel cars such as hot metal cars, cinder pots, and ingot buggies from the small staging yard to the various locations.

Operational possibilities are considerably enhanced when the layout is expanded with an additional 4x8 sheet (cut as shown in the cutting diagram). The extension adds a blooming mill as a destination for the ingots and also rolling mills for the pickup of finished products. With this design, the layout fits neatly in a corner of a 12x13 room, assuming a 2-foot aisle on the right for access to blast furnace row.

This design could also serve as a basis for further expansion depending on available space. Rolling mills and other facilities can be added to the layout where the slag dump is currently located.

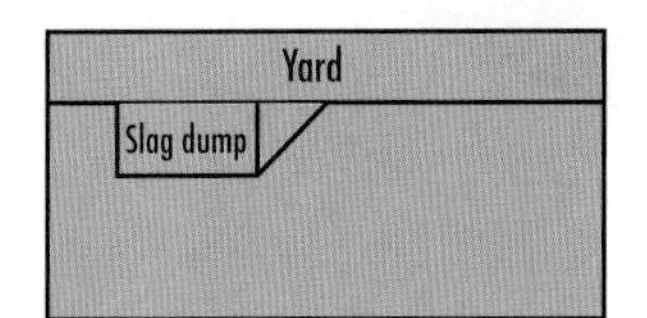

Plywood cutting diagram for extension (smaller scale than main drawing)

Coke hoppers wait in a yard in front of the blast furnaces at Detroit Steel.

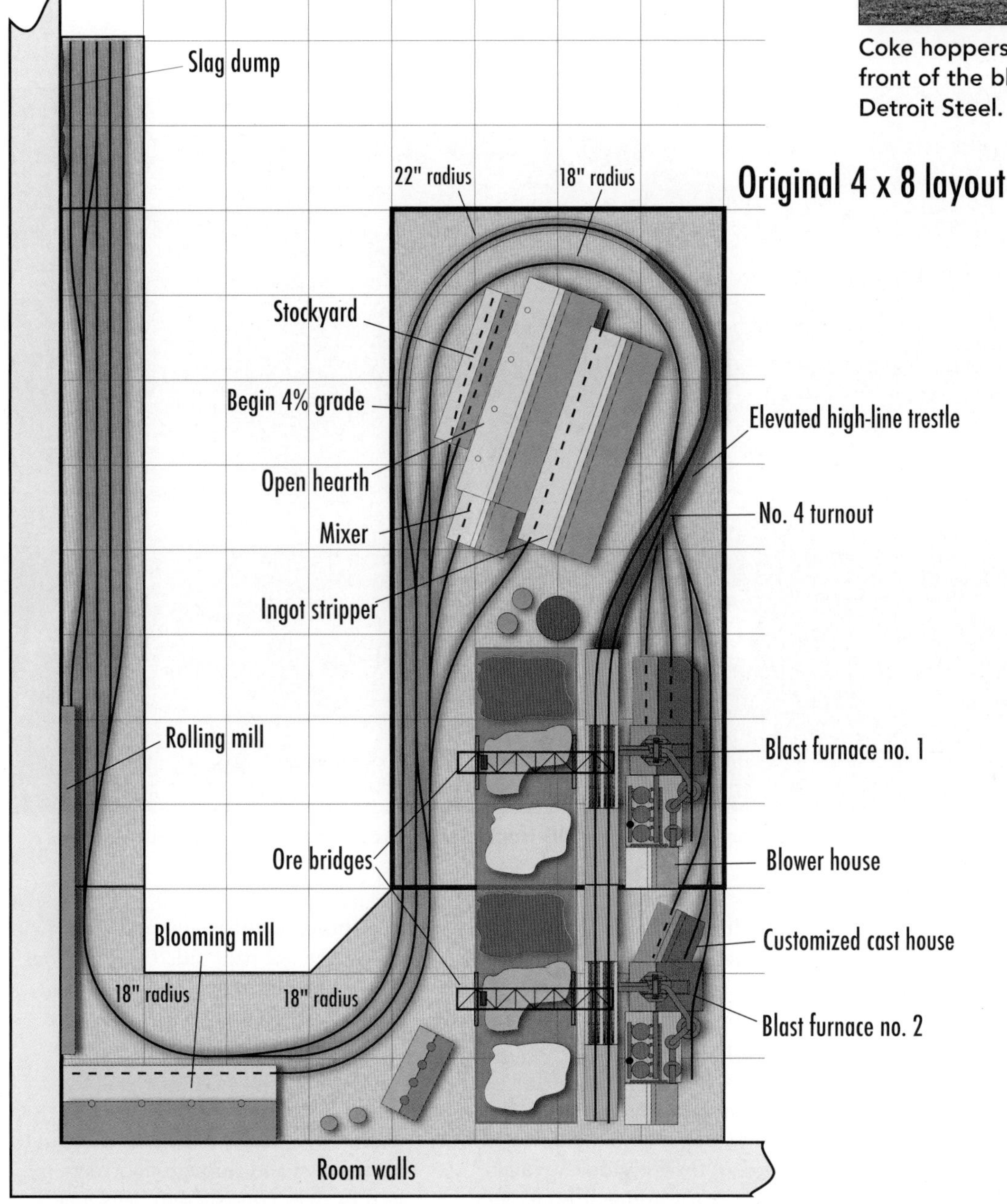

FIRST STEEL — HO scale

Size: 4 x 8, expanded to 10 x 13 feet
Prototype: Freelanced

Locale: Northeast United States
Era: 1950–1990
Style: Walk-in
Mainline run: 38 feet
Minimum radius: 18"

Turnouts: No. 6 (and one No. 4)
Maximum grade: 4 percent
Train length: 6–12 cars

Scale of plan: ½" = 1 foot, 12" grid

8

Keystone Viaduct

A brakeman rides the rear of a Western Maryland train as it pulls hopper cars from the truck load-out near Meyersdale. *Tom Biery*

Ntrak is a well-established and popular standard for modular model railroads. Its three-track standard makes for lots of crowd-pleasing model train action, but it can be hard to fit into a home layout. This Keystone Viaduct layout uses the three-track Ntrak lines to represent the Baltimore & Ohio on the Sand Patch Grade. Above those tracks is a small oval layout depicting the Western Maryland railroad as it crosses the B&O at Keystone Viaduct, just east of Meyersdale, Pennsylvania. The Keystone Viaduct is now part of a bicycle trail, but it still roars with heavy mountain traffic on this layout.

The idea of incorporating a separate layout on top of a elaborate Ntrak module was first pioneered by Matt Schaefer in the 1970s with his New River Module set. In addition to creating a dramatic scene, the separate upper layout allows the modeler to operate the layout at home without having the rest of the Ntrak layout present.

From an outside spectator's view, this layout shows an fairly accurate rendition of the Keystone Viaduct scene. The truss bridge is quite large and spans three tracks at an oblique angle. It was also built for double tracks, but only had one installed. Kitbashing or scratchbuilding the bridge is a fun challenge.

On the back side of the layout, a small freelanced town (named Schaefer in honor of Matt) allows for plenty of switching. It includes a mine and two passing sidings.

A tunnel on the right and a deep cut on the left help hide the WM oval loops. The Ntrak lines disappear into Sand Patch Tunnel on the right side.

The 3x6 modules are large, and transporting them requires a van or large SUV. Notching the corners makes them easier to negotiate up and down stairs and through doorways. Lightweight construction helps make them portable.

The Keystone and Sand Patch modules would make a fine home layout on their own. But if you wished, the sky is the limit in expansion as the B&O and WM paralleled each other for dozens of miles in southwestern Pennsylvania.

The expanded plan shown here features the Salisbury Viaduct and the Rockwood wye.

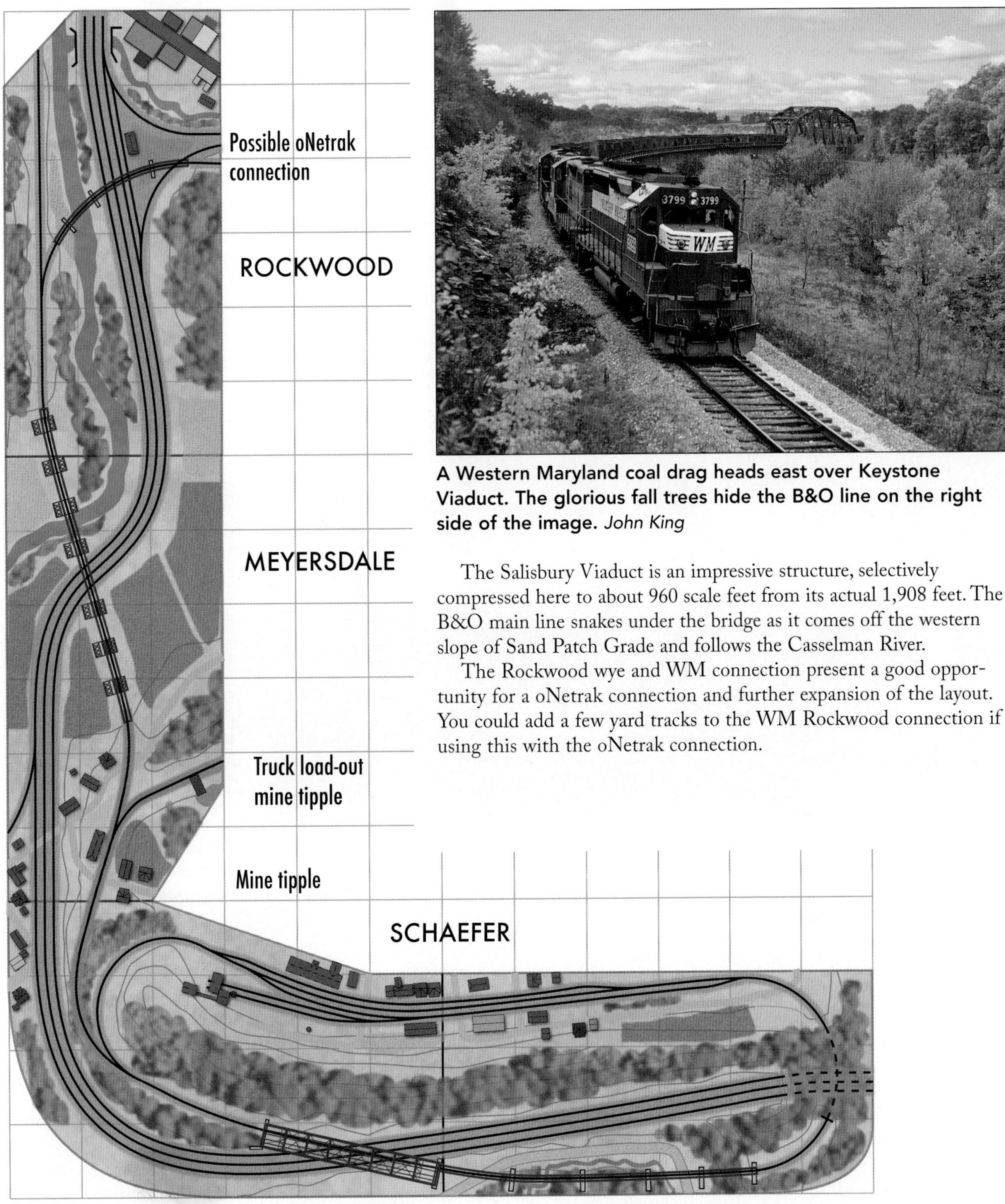

A Western Maryland coal drag heads east over Keystone Viaduct. The glorious fall trees hide the B&O line on the right side of the image. *John King*

The Salisbury Viaduct is an impressive structure, selectively compressed here to about 960 scale feet from its actual 1,908 feet. The B&O main line snakes under the bridge as it comes off the western slope of Sand Patch Grade and follows the Casselman River.

The Rockwood wye and WM connection present a good opportunity for a oNetrak connection and further expansion of the layout. You could add a few yard tracks to the WM Rockwood connection if using this with the oNetrak connection.

KEYSTONE VIADUCT — N scale

Size: 4 x 12 feet, expanded to 12 x 15
Prototype: WM, B&O

Locale: Meyersdale, Pennsylvania
Era: 1950–1970
Style: Modular
Mainline run: 24 feet
Minimum radius: 12" on WM, greater than 24" on Ntrak lines

Turnouts: No. 6
Maximum grade: 0 percent
Train length: 15–20 cars

Scale of plan: ½" = 1 foot, 12" grid

Brooke Yard

C&O C-6 no. 125, a 0-6-0, spent most of its career switching the Norfolk Brooke Yard. The buildings in the background are a wonderful jumble of gables, walls, and painted signs that add interest to modeled structures. *Courtesy of the Chesapeake & Ohio Historical Society*

Brooke Yard was an isolated pocket terminal in Norfolk, Virginia, served by the Chesapeake & Ohio Railway via car float. There was no rail connection on land.

I first wrote about Brooke Yard in an article for *Model Railroad Planning* in 2002. Over the years, several people have asked me about fitting that layout to different spaces in both N and HO scale. Here are two of the HO plans I developed in response to these requests.

The 7x11 plan had to fit a very odd-shaped space in a basement. There were doors on three sides of the space. The plan allows access to all the doors, although the gap to the bottom closet door is a little tight.

The 4x8 version is interesting because it is much more compressed, but it still manages to capture the spirit and operational flavor of the area.

Both plans utilize a wall on the river side to create an peninsula-style layout. The three open sides allow operator access. The wall could have a riverfront scene painted on it.

The car float in the larger design is about 4 feet long (scale 330 feet). Even at this length, it is about one car length shorter than the actual float. Nonetheless, it can hold about 20 cars, more than enough for an interesting switching session. The float in the smaller plan can hold 12 cars on two tracks.

Both plans provide ample room for ship models. Tramp steamers were frequent visitors to the ocean pier. There are several suitable models that can be used, including some in 1/96th scale. The smaller scale models should be just right as they would provide some forced perspective.

This yard had one engine assigned to it at a time. For much of the steam era, C&O C-6 no. 125, an 0-6-0, handled the switching chores. It was an Alco product inherited from the Hocking Valley. It served until 1951. Brass models of this engine may be available. If not, any of the fine-running plastic 0-6-0s could act as a stand-in. Models of small boxcab diesels are available for later era HO scale modelers.

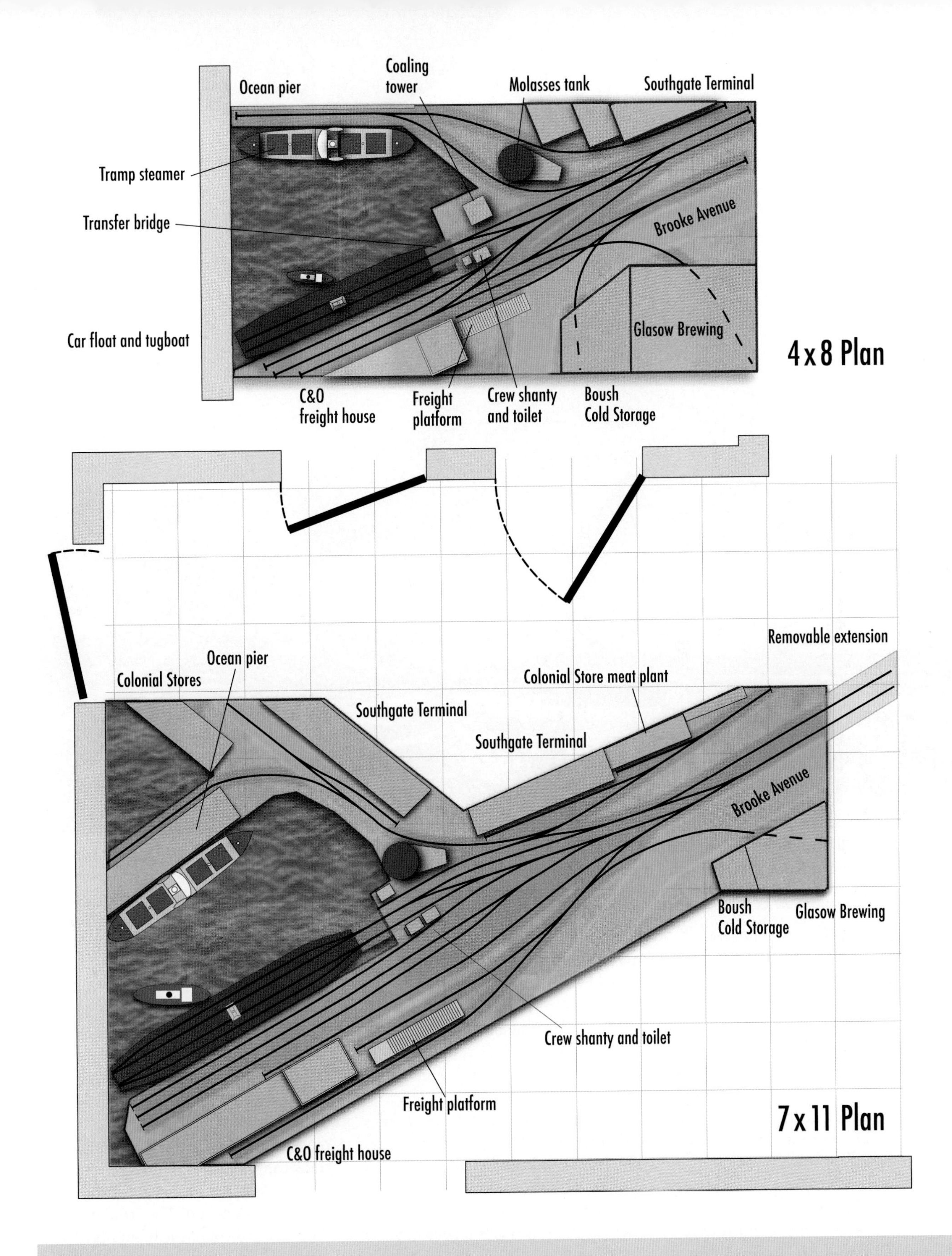

BROOKE YARD — HO scale

Size: 4 x 8 or 11 x 7 feet
Prototype: C&O

Locale: Norfolk, Virginia
Era: 1950–1955
Style: Peninsula
Mainline run: 11 feet
Minimum radius: 18"

Turnouts: No. 5
Maximum grade: 0 percent
Train length: 6–12 cars

Scale of plan: ½" = 1 foot, 12" grid

10

Overland Route

Workers install stone abutments for a permanent bridge over the Green River for the Union Pacific line through Wyoming. Citadel Rock stands in the distance. The Western Pacific and Central Pacific also worked on the line, which was known originally as the Pacific Railroad and later as the Overland Route. *Library of Congress*

Opened for through traffic on May 10, 1869, with the ceremonial driving of the Golden Spike at Promontory Summit, the nearly 2,000-mile transcontinental railroad cemented the union of states.

This layout commemorates that momentous event with a vignette-style design on a classic 4x8 footprint. It features three separate, somewhat fictionalized vignettes depicting activity just after the line opened.

The west side of the layout features the river harbor of Sacramento, California. Ships brought construction materials, freight, and passengers here to start the rail journey east. The layout has just enough room to include some HO scale ship models.

The next vignette features a free-lanced trestle across a steep canyon carved by the Truckee River in the Sierra Madre Mountains. The tracks curve through here on an 18" radius with an easement. This is not a problem for the small 4-4-0 engines and short freight cars that travel the layout.

The last vignette is a scene of the wide-open hill country of Wyoming, where the Bitter Creek River paralleled the railroad for much of its route. The fictionalized town is named Bitter Creek because it shares a deep cut with that river. A small town has sprouted up along the tracks. An early coal tipple is a harbinger of the massive coal industry that will develop near here. It also helps disguise the hole in the backdrop. The railroad has a small engine service facility here with a gallows turntable, water tank, and wood rick.

The layout packs a lot of action on a 4x8 because of the small size of 19th century railroad equipment and ships.

The track should be laid on rough wood ties. The turnouts should have stub points, which will probably have to be handlaid. However, all the turnouts are standard sizes, so commercial track can be used if desired.

The vignettes are separated by a three-part skyboard. The structure for the skyboard could easily support an integral lighting valance.

The blank face could reside against a wall, making the layout a three-sided peninsula. Expanding the layout would be possible by adding a siding to Bitter Creek that curves off to the left.

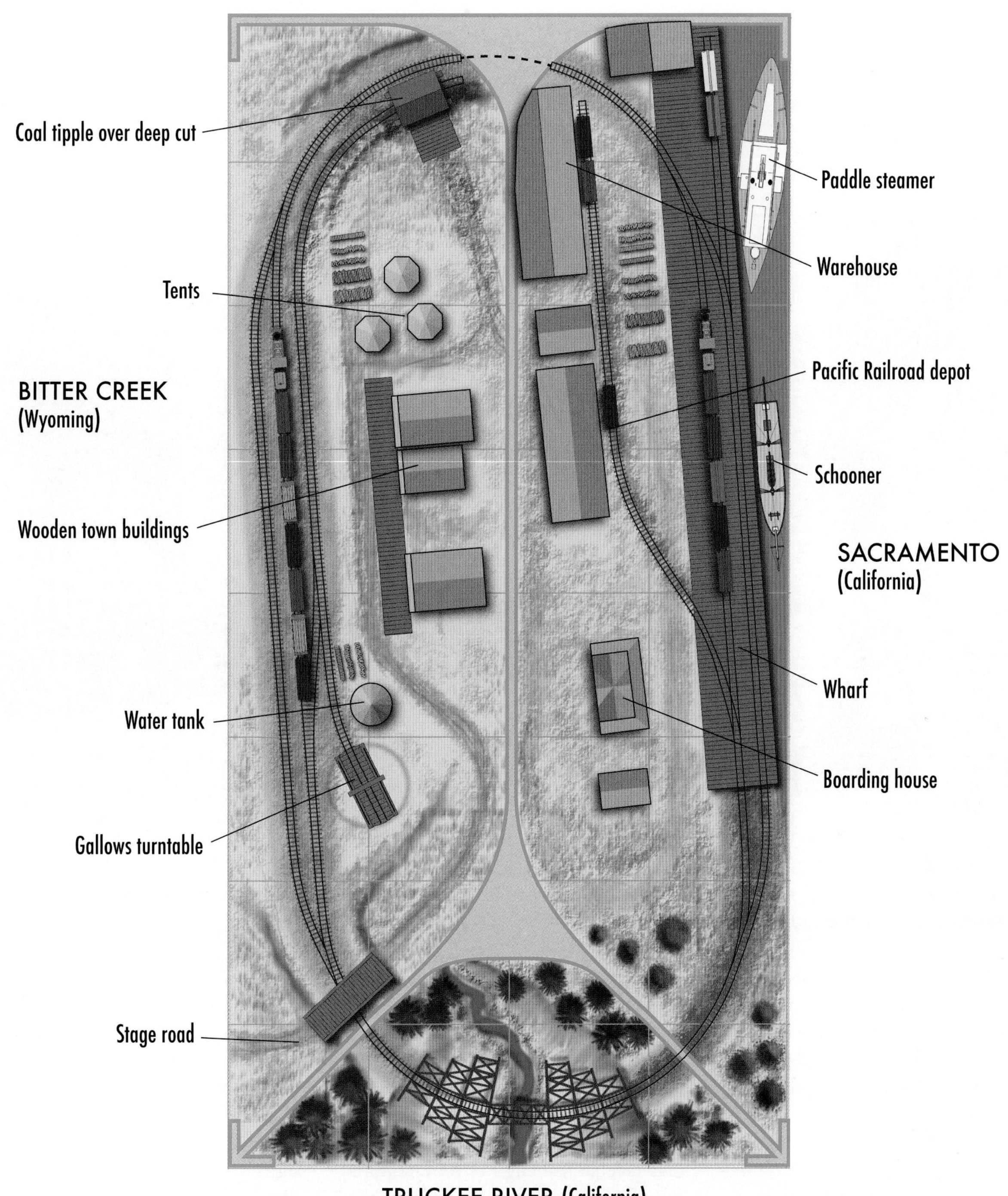

OVERLAND ROUTE — HO scale

Size: 4 x 8 feet
Prototype: CP, UP, WP

Locale: Wyoming and California
Era: 1869
Style: Island
Mainline run: 22 feet
Minimum radius: 18"

Turnouts: No. 6
Maximum grade: 0 percent
Train length: 6–8 cars

Scale of plan: 1" = 1 foot, 12" grid

Menil-La-Tour

A U.S. Army 2-6-2 Baldwin steamer runs down the street in the small French town of Cornieville, which is near the area depicted in this layout. *National Archives*

By spring of 1918, the United States had deployed enough combat troops to take over their own sectors of the front just southeast of the famous Verdun battlefields.

American railway troops operated standard and narrow gauge (60 centimeter) rail lines to supply the front.

The track plan depicts some of the American rail lines and logistic operations in an area about 20–30 kilometers behind the trenches near the city of Toul. Supplies and replacement soldiers arrived at Toul on standard gauge trains. Some transferred to narrow gauge trains for the ride to Menil-La-Tour. This was the regimental headquarters of the American railway engineers, as well as a narrow gauge railroad division point. It had a yard, engine service facility, shops, and barracks.

In the yard, the quartermaster corps trans-loaded cargo to cars according to their destinations. The engineers made up trains whose head-end power was determined by the destination. Gas mechanical engines were required to pull cars headed to the front, while cars departing for other safer locations could use steam engines. The steam engines, with their distinctive smoke and steam signatures, could not operate where enemy artillery could observe and reach them.

All these destinations are simulated in the fiddle yard. The layout operators build the outbound trains in the yard. They then head immediately to the fiddle yard under the disused meter gauge railway embankment. Empty trains head back to Toul. The actual rail network in this area was a complex web, and this layout vastly simplifies the operation to its essence.

Because Menil-La-Tour and Toul were far from the front, there are few signs of battle damage. Signs of civilian life trying to carry on are present, but the heavy military traffic and lack of local manpower meant farms and other industries were not producing at full capacity.

The canal and barge scene shows the contribution that the extensive French canal system made to supplying the war effort. It also provides the opportunity to build some interesting models and offers a location for switching cars.

An elevated embankment for an out-of-service meter gauge railway creates a backdrop for the U.S. Army 60cm gauge engine terminal at Menil-La-Tour. The line through the tunnel heads to the front lines. *National Archives*

MENIL-LA-TOUR — On30 or O14 scale

Size: 10 x 14 feet
Prototype: U.S. Army 12th Engineers
Locale: Menil-La-Tour, France
Era: 1918
Style: Shelf
Mainline run: 12 feet
Minimum radius: 18"
Turnouts: No. 6
Maximum grade: 0 percent
Train length: 10 cars

Scale of plan: ½" = 1 foot, 12" grid

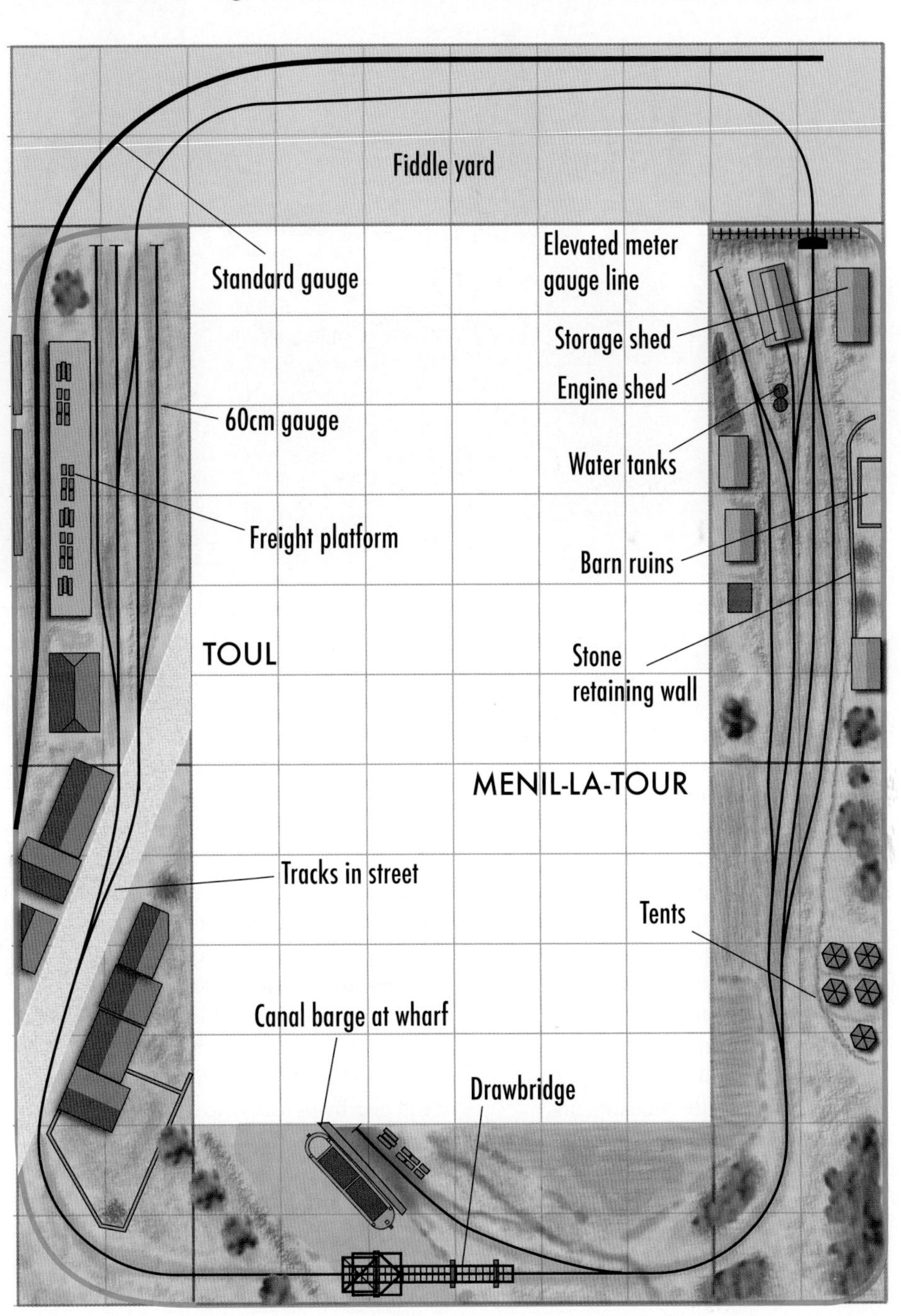

The layout can be built in On30 or the more prototypically correct O14. Kits are available for the gas mechanical engines (from the UK) and rolling stock (from France) that can be used in either gauge. Currently, no manufacturer makes a Baldwin 2-6-2 steam engine in this scale, although other steamers are available even if they are less appropriate for U.S. railway units in WWI. Kitbashing a HO mechanism to a Baldwin 2-6-2 is another approach if working in On30.

Some models of German rolling stock are also available. The Allies captured German equipment late in the war, so some German equipment, hastily repainted with U.S. markings, could run on the layout.

12

WWII Stateside Port

Longshoremen load a freighter, a U.S. Navy Landing Ship, Tank (LST), and a barge with Mk 6 landing craft in this postwar image in Seattle. Similar scenes occurred in most major United States ports during WWII. *National Archives*

Getting supplies, equipment, and men from the United States to WWII theaters of operation required a steady stream of ships. Axis U-boat activity forced the Allies to send their ships in large and heavily protected convoys. Railroad movements and stevedore operations revolved around loading these ships in time to meet their required convoy sailing date.

Railroad loading movements were quite intricate and required spotting of railcars alongside the ships in precise order and position, especially for railcars carrying vehicles or aircraft. These cars had to be precisely positioned so that the cranes could load the correct holds on the ship. They also had to be delivered in the correct sequence that supported the ship's loading plan.

The shelf layouts presented here (two variations) allow the layout operator to explore complex railcar switching with military cargoes.

The lower layout design places the ships between the aisle and the tracks. This allows more room for modeling the ships and lighters. The plan includes staging tracks hidden behind the 850-foot-long pier warehouse.

The upper plan flips the orientation of the pier by putting the ships along the backdrop. Instead of detailed ship models, the plan uses simple flat poster images of the ships. To help with the illusion, this version of the layout uses one wall of the warehouse to partially obscure the view of the two-dimensional ships. The railroad operator looks through the open doors of the warehouse to observe the railroad switching. The layout should be mounted near eye level so that the view of the two-dimensional ships is always through the open doors or the steel gantries on top of the pier warehouse (Section A-A). The pier should have magnetic uncoupling devices liberally deployed to allow remote uncoupling, as reaching over the warehouse to manually uncouple cars could be difficult.

To help create the atmosphere of wartime convoy loading, these small layouts can use three jobs: ship load master, yard master, and railroad crew. The ship load master provides the railroad yard master with a load plan and sequence. From that load plan, the yard master

This Pennsylvania Railroad wartime poster illustrates the type of action this layout attempts to re-create.
Library of Congress

WWII STATESIDE PORT — HO scale

Size: 10 x 12 feet
Prototype: Freelanced
Locale: United States port
Era: 1942–1945
Style: Shelf
Mainline run: 22 feet
Minimum radius: 18"
Turnouts: No. 5
Maximum grade: 0 percent
Train length: 8–12 cars

Scale of plan: 3⁄8" = 1 foot, 12" grid

creates switch lists. The engineers and conductors then use the switch list to spot the cars. The jobs of load master and yard master could be performed by the same individual. A session would start with empty cars on the pier tracks. The railroad crews pull the empties, and then they would spot the loads. Car types should include boxcars and flatcars with military vehicles or loads, and an occasional passenger train with crews and soldiers.

The switch crews shove the empties into staging as the yard master requires. With loads spotted, the train crew can then take a break while the ship load master takes the loads off the cars, creating empties to remove. Then the cycle repeats.

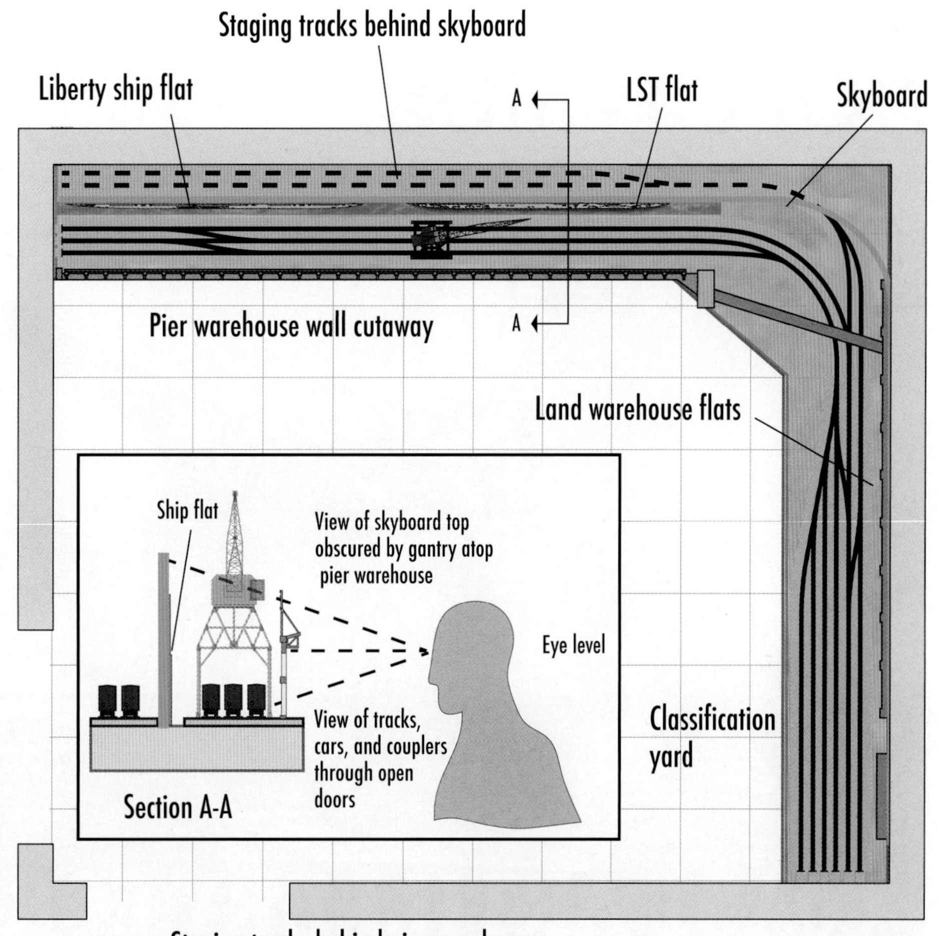

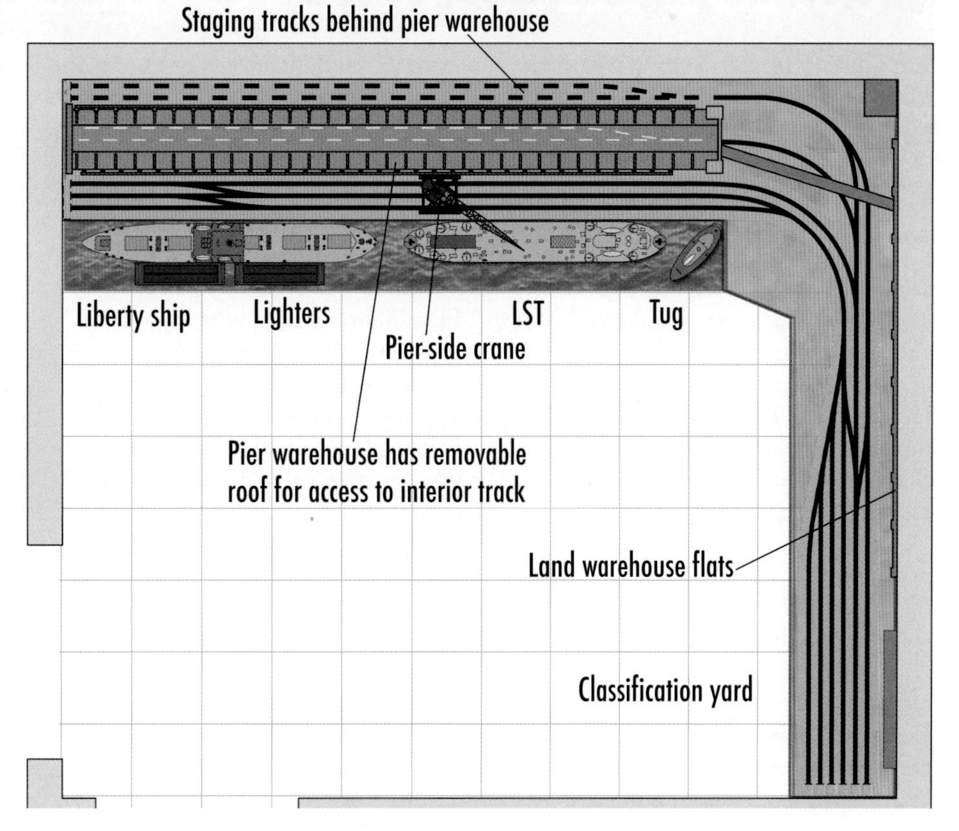

13

Fort Miles

A recruiting poster from WWII shows the crew of an 8-inch railway gun in the Coast Artillery Corps. The Fort Miles layout is set during the short period when these rail-based guns protected United States harbors from attack. *National Archives*

From the Revolutionary War to WWII, the United States built hundreds of forts with heavy artillery to defend its coast lines. The rise of long-range missiles and aircraft made these forts obsolete.

Fort Miles, on the tip of Cape Henlopen in Delaware, was one of the more interesting forts. The Army chose this location because it could protect the southern entrance to the Delaware River. Along with a comparable fort at Cape May, New Jersey, they protected the important industrial areas surrounding Philadelphia.

Built in 1938, Fort Miles utilized railway-mounted guns tucked in U-shaped temporary firing positions carved out of the sand dunes as well as an assortment of other nonrail mounted artillery. The Army laid a rail line into the area to bring in construction materials and to allow for the operation of 8-inch railway guns.

Initially, troops lived in tents, but the Army soon built more permanent structures for barracks, mess halls, training centers, storage areas, and theaters.

Unlike older forts that used stone or masonry, this fort initially used sand revetments to create the gun positions. Two thousand soldiers from Battery E, 52nd Artillery Regiment, and other units provided crews for the guns.

As the war progressed, units shuffled in and out of the fort, but construction work continued. The Army built concrete bunkers to house massive 16-inch cannons and tall observation towers for controlling and directing the guns' fire. Though the gun positions were abandoned soon after the war ended, many of the concrete structures still stand.

The guns of the fort never fired in anger, although German submarines sunk many Allied ships nearby. In May 1945, the German submarine U-858 surrendered to the soldiers in the fort.

The layout depicts the time between 1938 and 1942, when the guns were still in their temporary sand revetments and more elaborate concrete bunkers were under construction. Modeling this period allows you to run trains with construction materials as well as normal supply trains, troop trains, and artillery training specials.

The layout can be built on a shelf in a small room or be made as portable

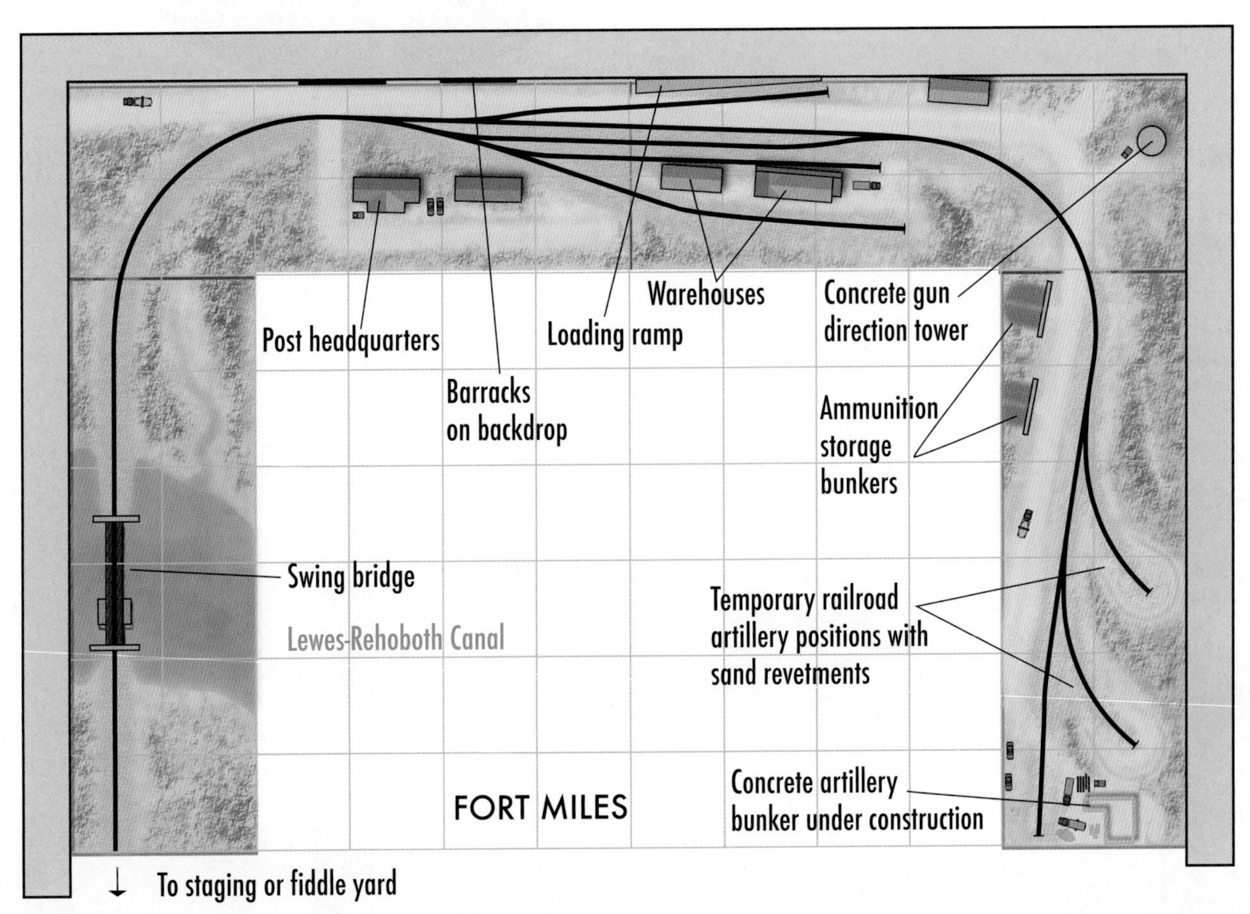

sections. The tracks connect at the lower left to staging that represents Queen Anne's Railway (a subsidiary of the Pennsylvania Railroad at this time).

The scenery consists of scrub brush on sand dunes. The wooden buildings follow standard U.S. Army designs and are relatively easy to scratchbuild. The 8-inch railway guns also require scratchbuilding. While being more complex to scratchbuild than the wooden buildings, they are relatively simple compared to larger railway guns.

The guns usually remained set up, but they were moved for maintenance or for training the crews. When emplaced, the guns were camouflaged with snow fences and other materials. However, the items must be removable if you wish to simulate moving the guns by railway during training specials.

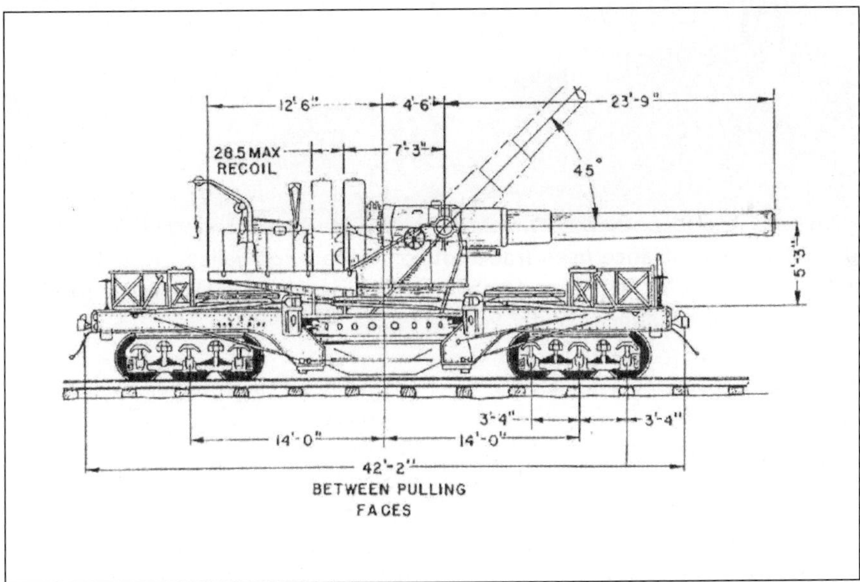

No commercial models of the Baldwin-built, 8-inch railway guns used at Fort Miles are available, although some similar models are available. Given that they are an important part of this layout, scratchbuilding two of these guns would be a priority task. *U.S. Army*

FORT MILES — HO scale

Size: 8 x 12 feet
Prototype: Fort Miles
Locale: Cape Henlopen, Delaware
Era: 1938–1942
Style: Shelf
Mainline run: 28 feet
Minimum radius: 24"
Turnouts: No. 5
Maximum grade: 0 percent
Train length: 5–8 cars

Scale of plan: ½" = 1 foot, 12" grid

14

Cape Canaveral

United Launch Alliance uses Trackmobiles to haul specialized RoadRailers and the mobile launch pad into position at Launch Complex 41, Cape Canaveral, Florida. Here, a U.S. Navy MUOS-2 satellite on an Atlas V rocket is getting ready to launch. *Walter Scriptunas*

When most model railroaders think about operations, they think about running and switching trains in accordance with a schedule. This little railroad based on Launch Complex 41 at Cape Canaveral also runs on a schedule, albeit one set by celestial mechanics.

In the 21st century, United Launch Alliance (ULA), a private contractor, launches the Atlas V rocket into orbit from this complex with U.S. Air Force and Navy satellites on board. The ULA crews assemble the Atlas V rockets vertically on a rail-mounted mobile launch platform in the Vertical Integration Facility (VIF) on the south side of the complex. About a day before launching, two Trackmobile locomotives push the mobile launch pad and its associated vans mounted on customized RoadRailers to the launch site. They withdraw before the rocket is launched, leaving the mobile launch pad at the launch site.

Launch Complex 41 is fairly compact, but some selective compression is still necessary. This plan uses two 7-foot-long sections to simulate the complex. One section houses the VIF, while the other hosts the launch pad. The layout design is sectional and portable so that it can be taken outside for launching model rockets from the launch pad.

DFR Technologies makes a flying model of the Atlas V rocket in a scale close to HO. It is detailed enough that it could be built as a static model, but that eliminates the fun of launching rockets from this unique model railroad.

BLI makes operating models of the Trackmobile. The RoadRailer vans can be kitbashed from Bowser models. You have to scratchbuild the mobile launch pad, simulating the four 250-ton railcars equipped with four sets of 4-axle roller-bearing trucks and hydraulic jacks. Making it from brass or other metal prevents damage from hot rocket exhaust during launches. The model VIF is 3.4 feet tall, an impressive model in its own right.

These two photos show the mobile launch pad and the RoadRailer vans at Launch Complex 41. The Atlas V rocket here has NASA's Maven, a Mars-bound spacecraft on board. *NASA*

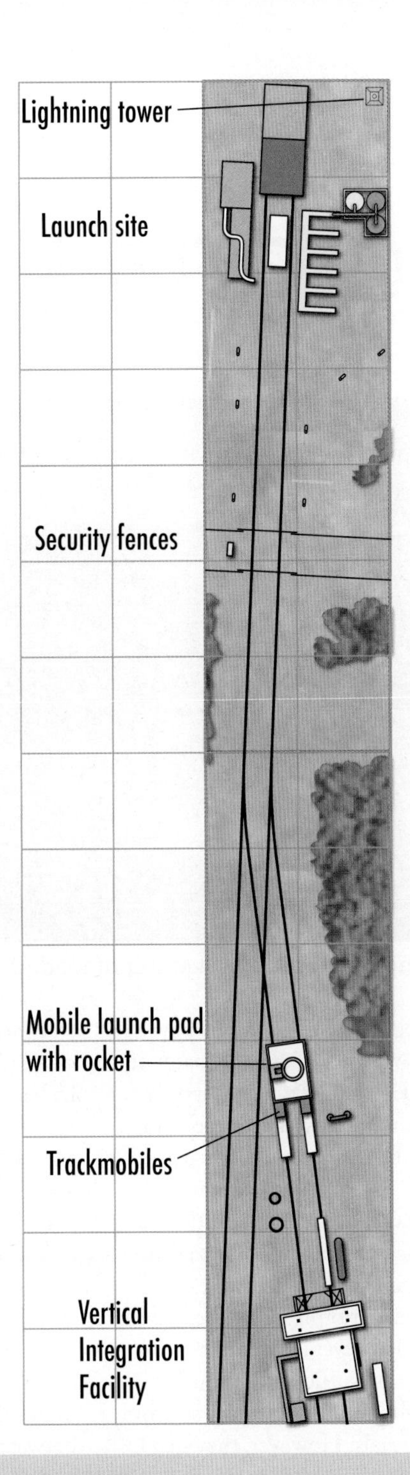

CAPE CANAVERAL — HO scale

Size: 2 x 14 feet
Prototype: ULA, NASA, USAF
Locale: Launch Complex 41, Cape Canaveral, Florida
Era: 2015
Style: Sectional, portable
Mainline run: 12 feet
Minimum radius: 40"
Turnouts: No. 6
Maximum grade: 0 percent
Train length: 2 special cars

Scale of plan: ½" = 1 foot, 12" grid

15

Victoria Crater Railway

This concept sketch shows a string of loaded ore cars at the mine load-out on the Victoria Crater Railway on Mars.

Recent rover expeditions have shown that Mars has many of the ingredients necessary for mankind's expansion beyond Earth. With manned missions being planned by several organizations, humans may land on Mars in the not-too-distant future. Colonization could happen soon thereafter.

In the scenario presented here, Mars has developed several settlements that are largely self-sufficient, producing air, water, food, fuel, and housing from native materials. However, they need to import finished high-technology products from Earth.

In return, they export Deuterium, a material needed in fission and fusion reactors. It is 10,000 times more valuable than gold, and is much more plentiful on Mars than on Earth. (This scenario is based largely on the ideas presented by Robert Zubrin in his book *The Case for Mars.*)

Early iron manufacturing on Mars used surface scrapers to mine the low-grade, iron-bearing soil. While it did produce enough iron to bootstrap the steel and other industries, the discovery of a rich vein of hematite "blueberries" in Victoria Crater led Martian business interests to begin mining there. Since the soil leading to the crater was not suitable for extensive heavy-wheeled vehicle traffic, the mining company built a narrow gauge railroad from the closest settlement, Musk, about 70 miles away, to haul the ore.

In exploring the right-of-way, the surveyors discovered a frozen lake under the loose soil about halfway between the crater and Musk. The mining company erected an electrolysis plant to convert the ice to hydrogen and oxygen. This creates hydrogen for fuel, oxygen for air to breathe, and Deuterium for export.

The model railroad layout is designed for a small room, but it could also be used as a portable layout to exhibit at train shows and science fairs It has three main areas, each built on a 6-foot-long section.

On the right side of the layout is the settlement of Musk with its industrial, agricultural, and cultural areas. Most of the structures can be depicted on the backdrop, but a passenger station and some industrial structures can be modeled, including a steel mill, chemical plant, and various manufacturing facilities. The steel mill uses a direct-reduction technique suitable for Martian conditions. The passenger station includes an airlock that allows passengers to board or exit the cars.

The tracks continue to the center section, which houses the electrolysis plant. The plant uses both photovoltaic cells and a fusion reactor to generate electricity. Here, a passing siding can be used to load tank cars with water, hydrogen fuel, and oxygen.

At the far left, the tracks reach the iron mine, a passenger station, and some smaller temporary housing units for workers. The station has an overlook for viewing mine activities and admiring the huge crater.

The mine is located in the crater. The bucket wheel excavators and a central benefactor device, depicted on the backdrop, extract ore from the exposed soil in the crater. The ore is sent to a tipple at the rim of the crater via conveyors. The tipple loads the ore into jimmies on two parallel loading tracks. There is no runaround, so the engines utilize a push-pull method of operation.

Since high-technology goods need to be imported from Earth, they are quite expensive. Thus, the railroad utilizes simple, rugged technology built as quickly and inexpensively as possible. This is the perfect situation for a narrow gauge railroad. In fact, from a distance, this railroad looks a lot like one on Earth 100 years earlier.

This makes the job of the modeler easier, as existing HO engines and cars can be used with only cosmetic alterations to account for operation in an atmosphere without oxygen. HO scale model diesels could be modified to have airtight operator compartments and hydrogen fuel tanks.

HO freight cars could be used with modifications such as removing the air brakes and perhaps lightening the frames. The reduced gravity on Mars means that cars will cube out before being overloaded by weight. A modeler in the United States could use European or Australian rolling stock, which is not often seen here, to create an exotic Martian look.

The track would use lightweight rail on concrete ties, as there is no wood on Mars.

By modeling in S scale, you could use 28mm scale science-fiction figures from various manufacturers. These companies also make futuristic vehicles that can help detail the scenes. On Mars, the figures must wear spacesuits. However, recent research at MIT and other places is leading to the creation of spacesuits that resemble wet suits, which would be more comfortable to wear. So converting these S scale figures to having these new spacesuits may be easily done with a little modeling putty.

All structures need to be scratchbuilt, and you can use HO scale industrial parts like tanks and electric towers. Mars colonization literature suggests that structures would be comprised of domes and modular elements, or made from locally fabricated bricks. Many housing units and structures would be built at least partially underground for protection from radiation. However, agricultural units would need exposure to sunlight, possibly through transparent domes.

Operating the layout is rather simple. Trains with ore cars and tank cars shuttle back and forth to the various industries. Other trains take passengers and workers to and fro.

The ore shuttle can be animated for simplified operation when displaying at shows. The operator would be free to interact with the spectators to discuss the potential benefits and costs of settling Mars.

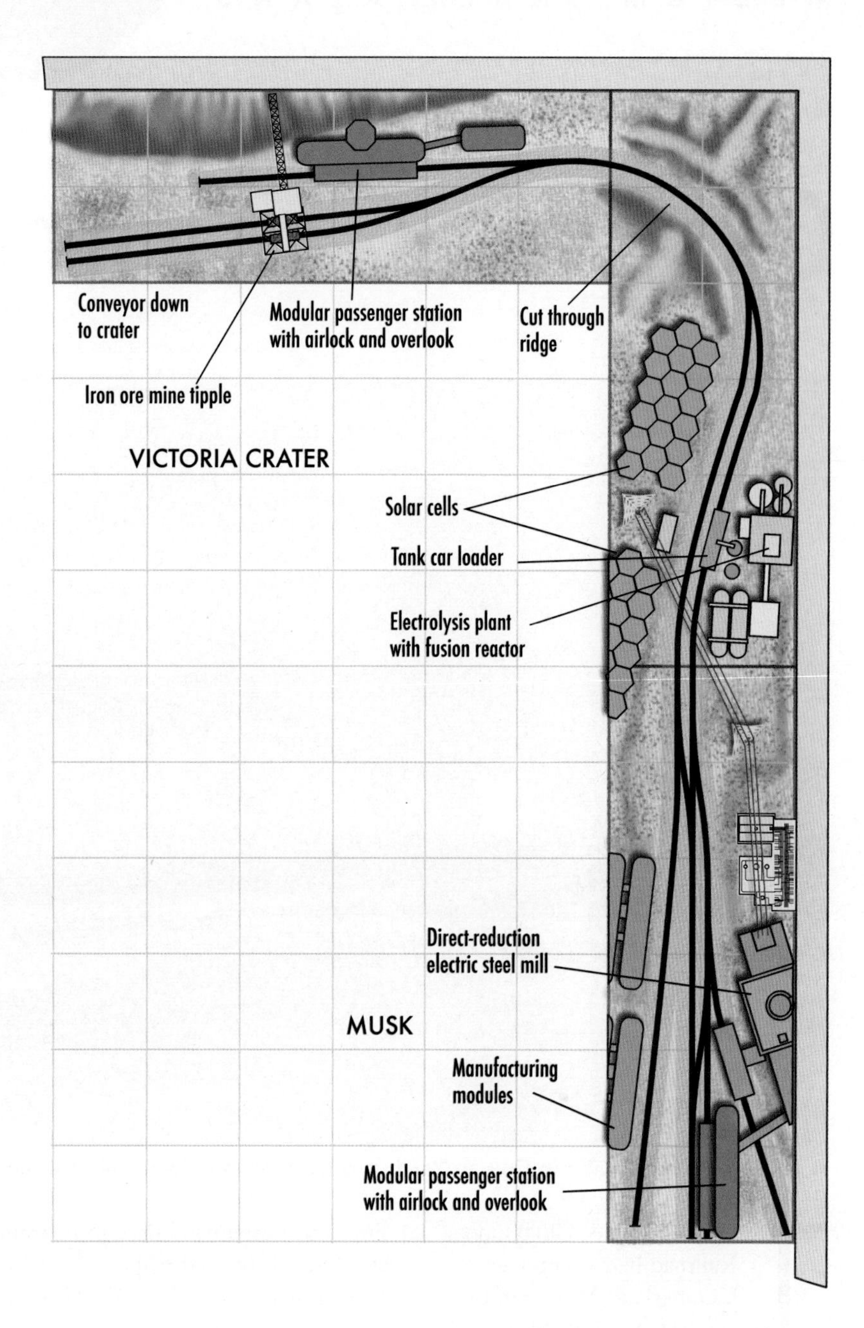

VICTORIA CRATER RAILWAY — Sn30 scale

Size: 8 x 12 feet
Era: 2080–2100
Locale: Mars
Prototype: Freelanced
Style: Shelf or exhibition
Mainline run: 18 feet
Minimum radius: 24"
Turnouts: No. 6
Maximum grade: 0 percent
Train length: 4–6 cars

Scale of plan: ½" = 1 foot, 12" grid

Cowan Country

A CSX helper set waits in Cowan Yard. A device on no. 505's pilot allows uncoupling on the fly. *Mike Spoor*

The Nashville & Chattanooga Railroad had to conquer Cumberland Mountain to connect its namesake cities. From its construction until today, the line has featured helper operations. The 2.35 percent grade starts just south of Cowan, Tennessee, and extends for 2.5 miles to the summit tunnel. On the south side, the grade is steeper (2.5 percent) and longer (4.5 miles).

The Tracy Branch departs the main line at the mountain's base and climbs even more steeply, and eventually passes over the main on a bridge just north of the Cumberland Mountain tunnel. The branch was abandoned in the 1980s.

This multideck N scale layout is set in the 1970s when the Tracy Branch still had traffic and Louisville & Nashville owned the main line. The line is still used by CSX, and its trains still frequently need helpers.

The layout main line climbs out of Cowan to the summit at the tunnel. Then it drops to Sherwood. There is ample room for staging under Cowan and the central peninsula.

The Tracy Branch climbs at 4 percent grade and ends up about 11" above the descending line to Sherwood. A helix connects the staging to the north end of Cowan.

Operations focus on mainline trains, most of which need helpers. Switching occurs at Cowan and the cement plant.

The helpers cut off at the summit and return. Helpers may be needed in both north and south directions.

A local turn can head up the Tracy Branch to work the mines and industries there.

COWAN COUNTRY — N scale

Size: 12 x 20 feet
Prototype: L&N, CSX
Locale: Cowan, Tennessee
Era: 1970s
Style: Multideck
Mainline run: 90 feet
Minimum radius: 18" on main line, 15" on Cowan wye
Turnouts: No. 6
Maximum grade: 2.5 percent on main line, 4 percent on branch line
Train length: 20–30 cars

Scale of plan: ¼" = 1 foot, 12" grid

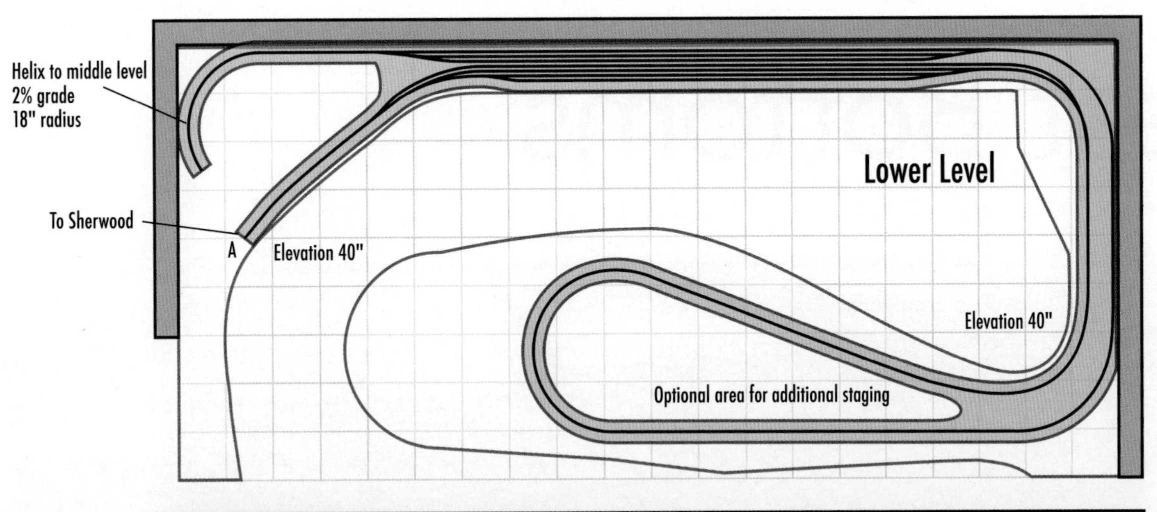
Helix to middle level
2% grade
18" radius
To Sherwood
A
Elevation 40"
Lower Level
Elevation 40"
Optional area for additional staging

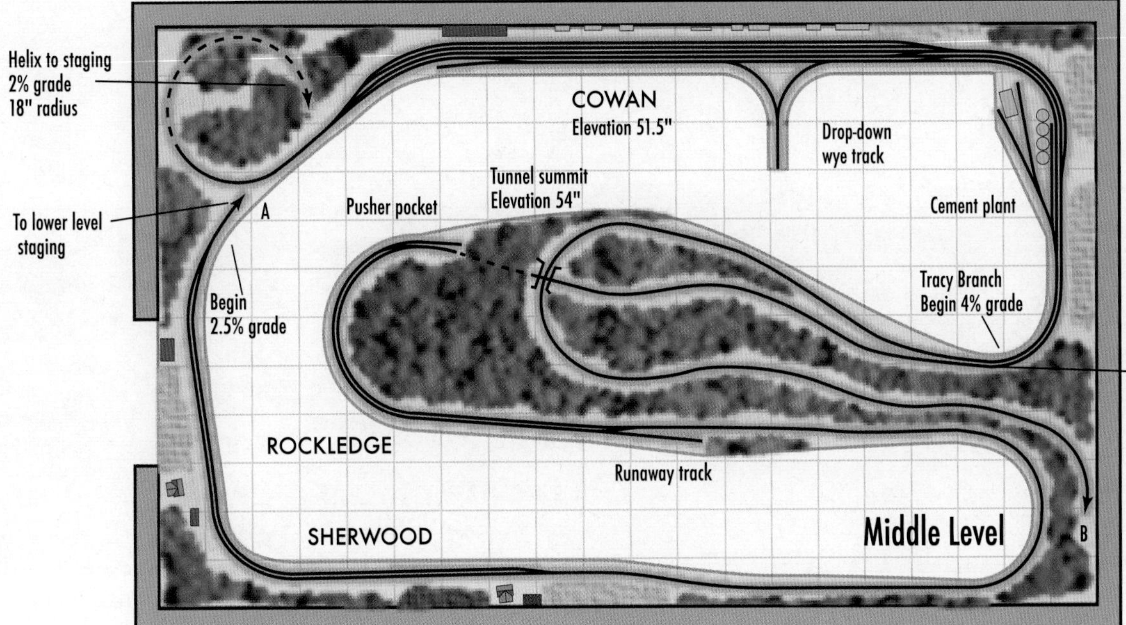
Helix to staging
2% grade
18" radius
COWAN
Elevation 51.5"
Drop-down
wye track
Tunnel summit
Elevation 54"
Pusher pocket
To lower level
staging
A
Cement plant
Tracy Branch
Begin 4% grade
Begin
2.5% grade
Main line
Begin 2.0% grade
Elevation 51.5"
ROCKLEDGE
Runaway track
To Tracy Branch
on upper level
Elevation 65"
SHERWOOD
Middle Level
B

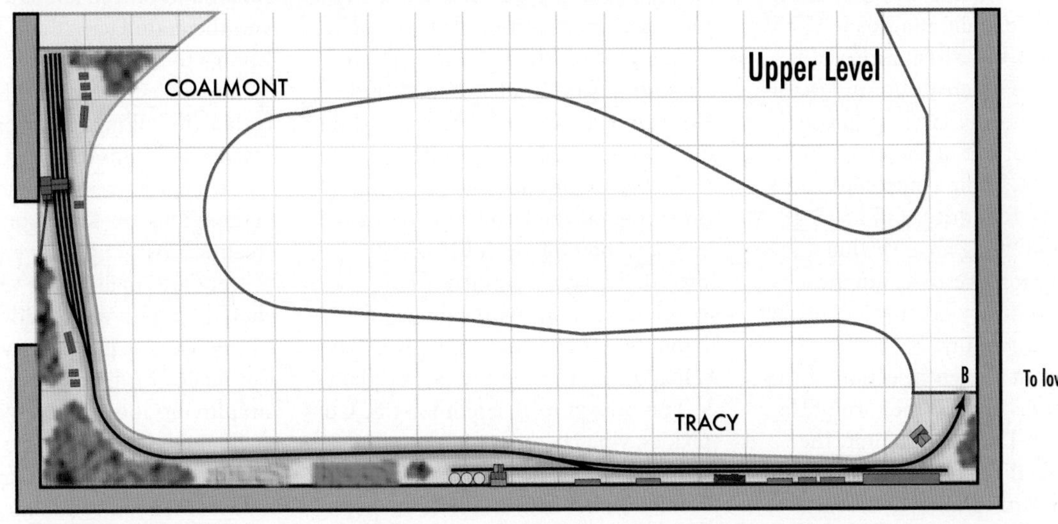
COALMONT
Upper Level
B
To lower level
TRACY

17

West Bottoms

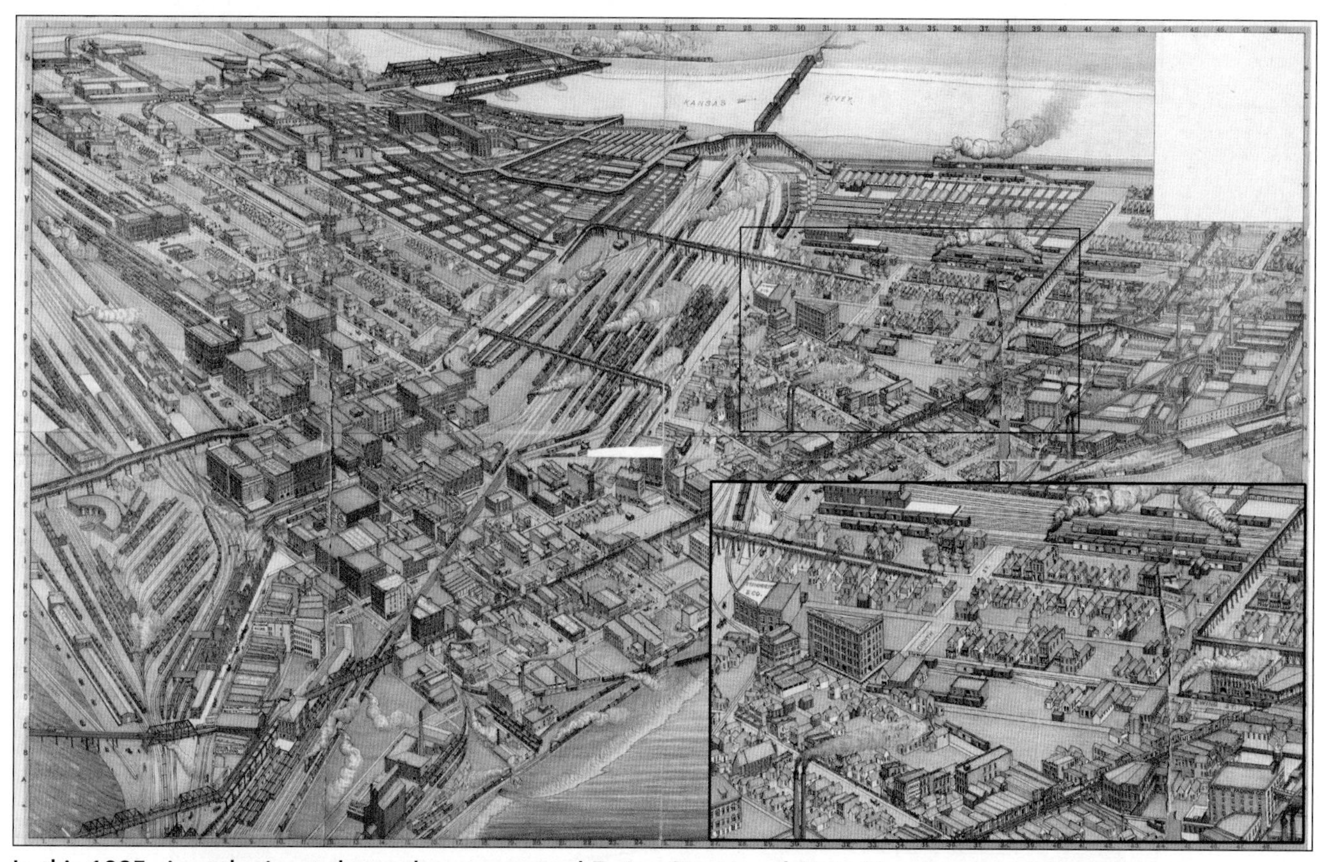

In this 1895 view, the inset shows the area around Ewing Street and State Line Road. *Library of Congress*

In 1869, the Hannibal & St. Joseph Railroad Co. built a railroad bridge over the Missouri River at Kansas City to create an important transportation hub. Twelve railroad lines soon shot out of the newly built Union Depot. Grain companies, lumberyards, foundries, and housing filled the low-lying area. Within a few years, a thriving livestock and meat-processing industry became a core part of the city's economy.

This layout depicts a section of the West Bottoms around the turn of the 20th century. During this time, the Missouri Pacific served industries from a large rail yard running at an angle to the streets. That yard is depicted in the upper left corner with mostly dummy tracks. A siding peels off the one live main yard track and heads to a small sorting yard on the right side. Behind the sorting yard is a large stockyard, shown mostly on the backdrop. Adding appropriate smells is optional.

The Armour Packing Co. at the lower edge of the layout was a vast complex, too large to fully model. Instead, the layout simulates rail service to Armour with sidings on Ewing Street and State Line Road as well as a coal trestle for a power plant.

The sidings to A. Steinhorst & Co. (pickles, vinegar, sauerkraut) and Joseph Schlitz Brewing are flipped in orientation because of a lack of space. Thus, the runaround in the sorting yard is important because there is no runaround on the left side of the layout and there are facing- and trailing-point sidings to serve.

An appealing aspect of this era is that the rolling stock tends to be smaller than more modern equipment. Typical freight cars are 34 feet and engines are 4-4-0s or other small steamers. Although the engines of this era are small, being O scale, they should operate well. With just a few locomotives required, they are good candidates for battery power, thus simplifying the layout wiring.

The relatively simple track plan (with a small number of cars) also makes it a good candidate for conversion to Prototype 48 if you desire more realism.

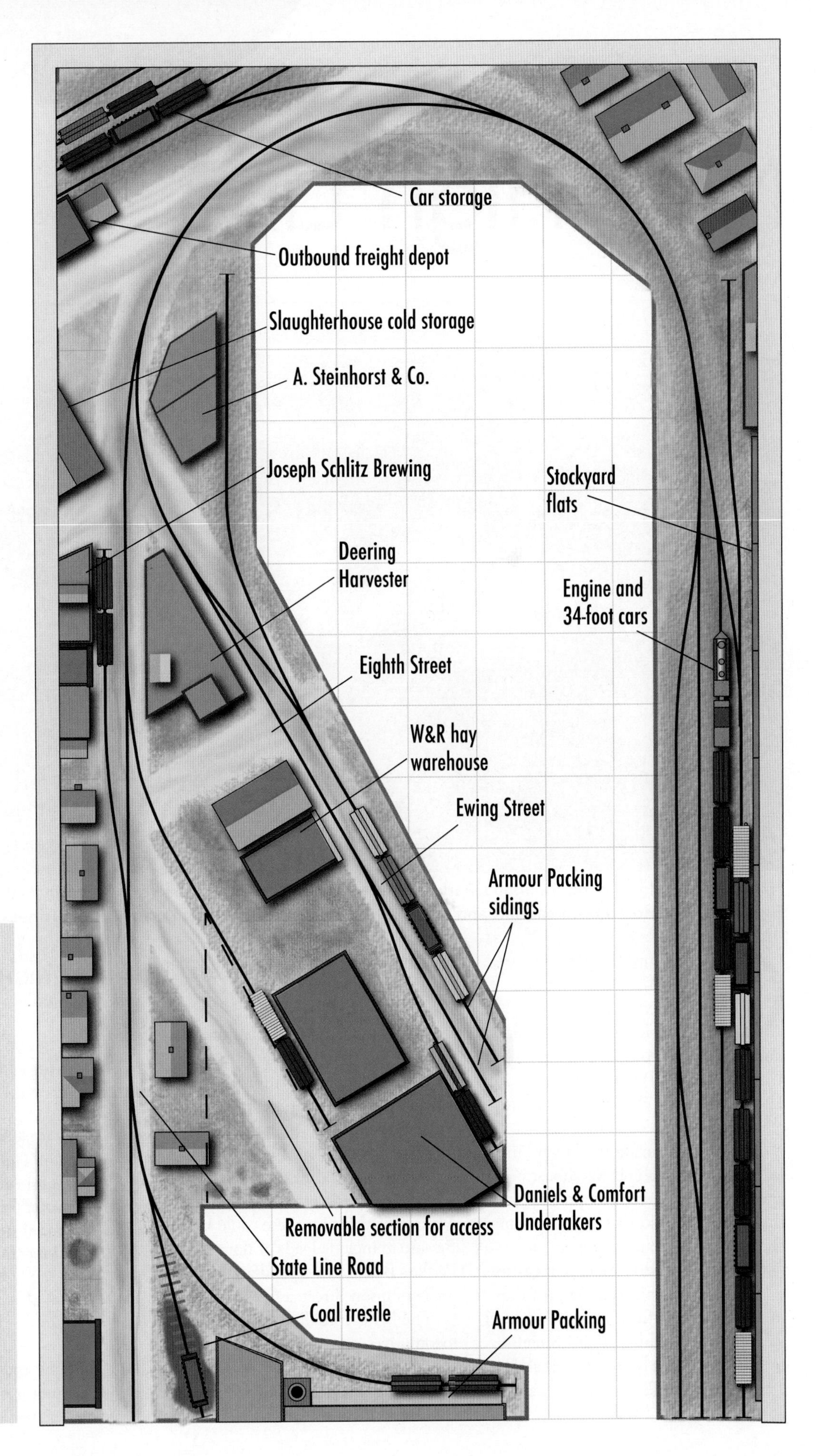

WEST BOTTOMS — O scale

Size: 10 x 20 feet
Prototype: Missouri Pacific
Locale: Kansas City, Missouri
Era: 1895–1903
Style: Walk-in
Mainline run: 48 feet
Minimum radius: 48"
Turnouts: No. 5
Maximum grade: 0 percent
Train length: 5–10 cars

Scale of plan:
½" = 1 foot, 12" grid

18

NYC High Line

Named after a local park, St. John's Park freight terminal with eight stub tracks terminated the south end of the High Line. It handled both carload and less-than-carload freight for numerous local business. *New York Central*

Going into the 20th century, New York Central trains traveled at grade level alongside pedestrians and horse-drawn wagons on city streets. City, state, and NYC officials agreed in 1929 to build an elevated railway and eliminate 105 street-level crossings.

Trains began using the High Line in 1934. Factories and warehouses along the way moved shipping docks to the upper floors so that raw and manufactured goods could come and go without causing street-level congestion.

The layout depicts the High Line in 1951, starting from the ground-level staging yard at Thirty-Third Street to St. John's Park freight terminal. In 1951, this was still an industrial and commercial area. Meat packing, light industry, wholesale grocer, bakery, dairy, electronics, garment, and trucking concerns all resided here.

Larger industries received rail service direct to their facilities. On the layout, these include National Biscuit, Manhattan Refrigerating, Spear & Co., R. C. Williams, and the U.S. Post Office's Morgan Parcel Post Building.

Thousands of other customers received deliveries at the terminal. Making waybills for these could be fun. Be sure to include loads of flour for Perillo's Bakery (my grandfather's bakery on Thompson Street, a few blocks away).

The NYC initially ran boxcab steam locomotives on the High Line, but in the 1950s, the NYC also used RS3 diesels. Just about any boxcar or reefer could be found on the line.

NYC HIGH LINE — HO scale

Size: 12 x 20 feet
Prototype: New York Central
Locale: New York City
Era: 1951
Style: Walk-in
Mainline run: 60 feet
Minimum radius: 18"
Turnouts: No. 6
Maximum grade: 2 percent
Train length: 10–12 cars

Scale of plan: ½" = 1 foot, 12" grid

Building the elevated portions of the line requires either scratchbuilding or some clever kitbashing.

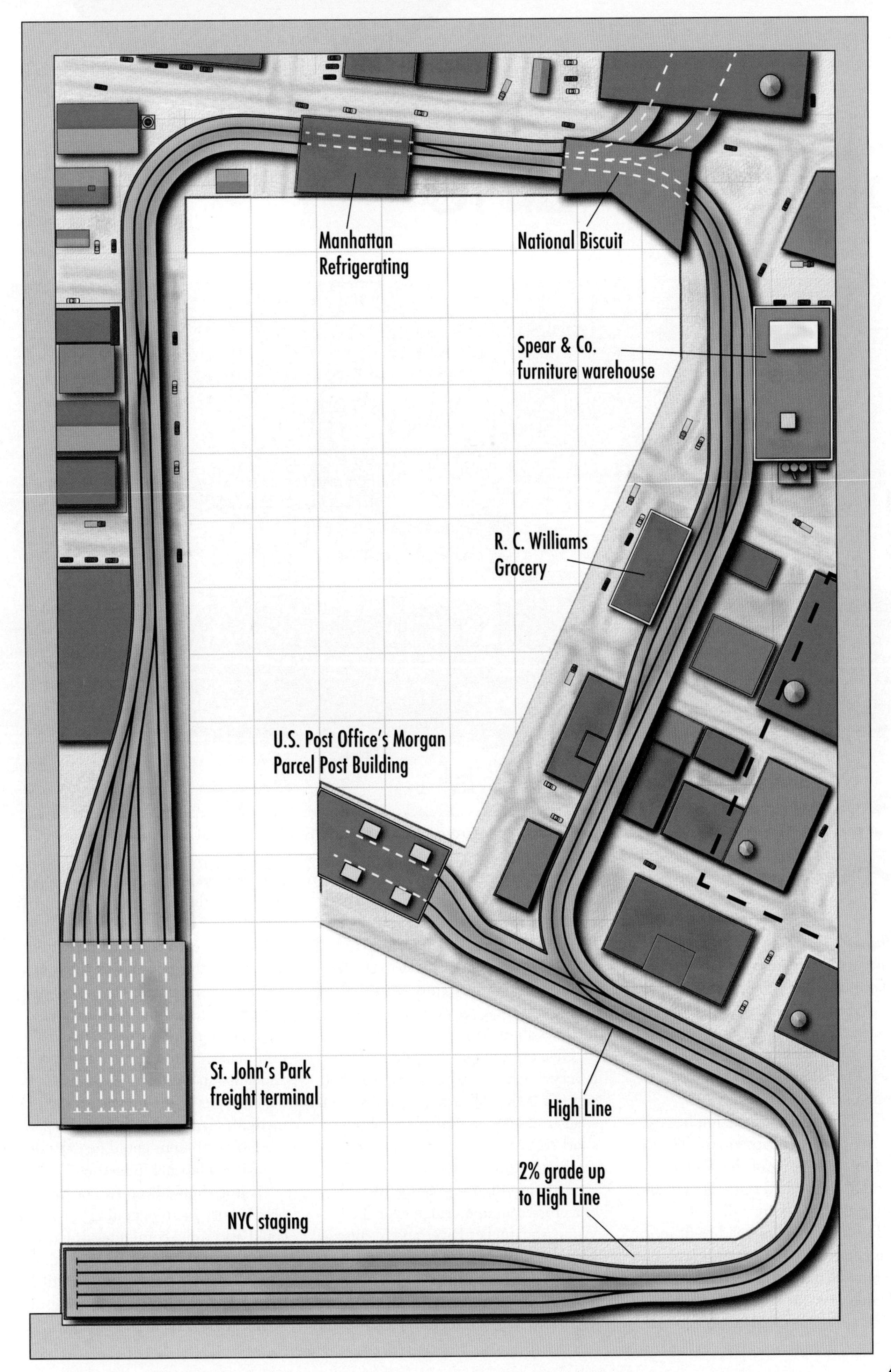
Manhattan
Refrigerating
National Biscuit
Spear & Co.
furniture warehouse
R. C. Williams
Grocery
U.S. Post Office's Morgan
Parcel Post Building
St. John's Park
freight terminal
High Line
2% grade up
to High Line
NYC staging

19

SNE Air Line

Ayer Mill at Lawrence, Massachusetts, serves as a prototype for this New England layout. *Library of Congress*

Charles Hays, president of the Grand Trunk Railway, conceived the Southern New England Railway. He wanted an alternate route to reach the coast of southern New England that avoided the rival New Haven Railroad. Chartered in 1910, it was to be an *air line* (a route with few grades, achieved by constructing long bridges, and numerous cuts and fills).

Grading and construction began, but the project collapsed after Hays died in the sinking of the *Titanic*. Some of the graded right-of-way and bridge abutments are still visible.

This layout is designed to fit in the basement of a typical townhouse. The open room has stairs descending on the left side. (At the lower left, the plan allows space for family use).

The freelance design imagines what SNE's terminal branch to Field's Point, south of Providence, might have looked like. At Wanskuck Junction, it veered off the SNE main line that was to go the union station in the center of downtown. The layout's staging yard represents all the lines above Wanskuck Junction.

Given the modest space, the plan is very much selectively compressed. It serves a large mill, a wharf, and several smaller industries. The plan includes a short section of street running before reaching the terminal yard.

After leaving the staging, the line crosses a large bridge over the Woonasquatucket River and a causeway over a small pond, reflecting the "air line" attitude of the builders.

Providence was known for its many mills, and the plan includes a large mill at Cranston. It is modeled as a low relief structure along the backdrop. It is typical of the large mills that were built in the early 20th century when coal, not water power, was the source of energy. A coal trestle serves the mill's powerhouse, and the mill features a loading spur and a storage track. The mill makes cotton textiles and receives and ships its products in boxcars.

The spur at the upper left serves a medium-sized screw factory. If space is available, this spur could be extended to serve additional industries.

Traffic should keep two or three people busy in an operating session. You could also run a commuter or passenger train to add variety to the operations. The commuter train would run from the SNE depot with flag stops at Cranston and Woonasquatucket.

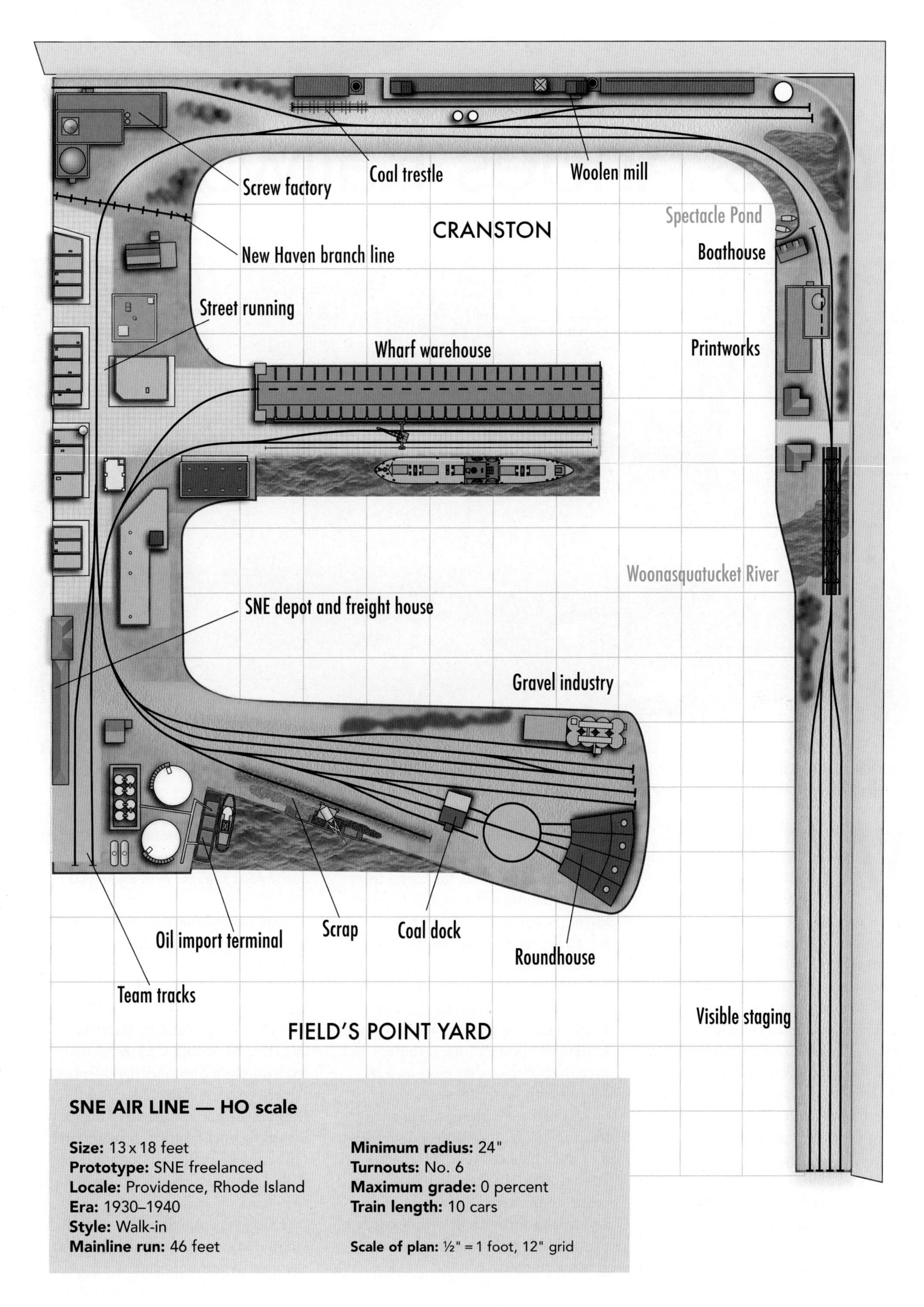

SNE AIR LINE — HO scale

Size: 13 x 18 feet
Prototype: SNE freelanced
Locale: Providence, Rhode Island
Era: 1930–1940
Style: Walk-in
Mainline run: 46 feet

Minimum radius: 24"
Turnouts: No. 6
Maximum grade: 0 percent
Train length: 10 cars

Scale of plan: ½" = 1 foot, 12" grid

20

Trans-Andes Railway

Two GE C30-7 diesels lead a Ferrocarril Central Andino train uphill at the Peunte Infiernillo in Peru. The nearly vertical canyon walls would make an impressive entry scene for the layout. *David Gubler*

With brightly painted, heavy-duty GE diesels hauling short trains over switchbacks, spiral tunnels, steep grades, and impressive bridges, the Ferrocarril Central Andino (FCCA) in Peru is a interesting railroad for modeling.

The second-highest railway in the world (with China's completion of its line to Tibet in 2005), it reaches 15,807 feet above sea level and links the Pacific port of Callao and the capital city of Lima with Huancayo and Cerro de Pasco in the central valley.

In July 1999, a consortium led by American Railroad Development Corp. took over operation of the railroad for the Peruvian government. Under this management team, traffic has been increasing, with 25 on-line customers shipping about 2 million tons per year.

The layout depicts the climb from San Bartolomé to the summit. Upon leaving staging, the trains enter the mountain town of San Bartolomé. Here, a single switchback requires the crews to turn the engine on an manual turntable and run around the train. From there, the grade is about 4 percent as the line climbs through tunnels and over steel bridges that cross a steep canyon with vertical walls.

Just before reaching the mining town of Casapalca, the layout zig-zags up a switchback. The mountains wrap around the train crew in this area to create an immersing scene. A mine and smelter operation, with brightly painted blue buildings, at Casapalca gets rail service.

The line continues climbing to the summit tunnel and reaches the yard and wye at Galera, with an elevation of 15,400 feet.

Just around the curve is a second large mine. The main line continues into a tunnel and down a helix to return to staging located under Casapalca.

The railroad runs an assortment of GE C30-7s and C39-8 locomotives purchased second-hand from American companies. Many of the freight cars are also American types including coal hoppers, boxcars, and tank cars. Cement, mining products, and supplies are the main commodities they haul.

Due to the switchbacks, the train lengths are short, about half of what the prototype would run.

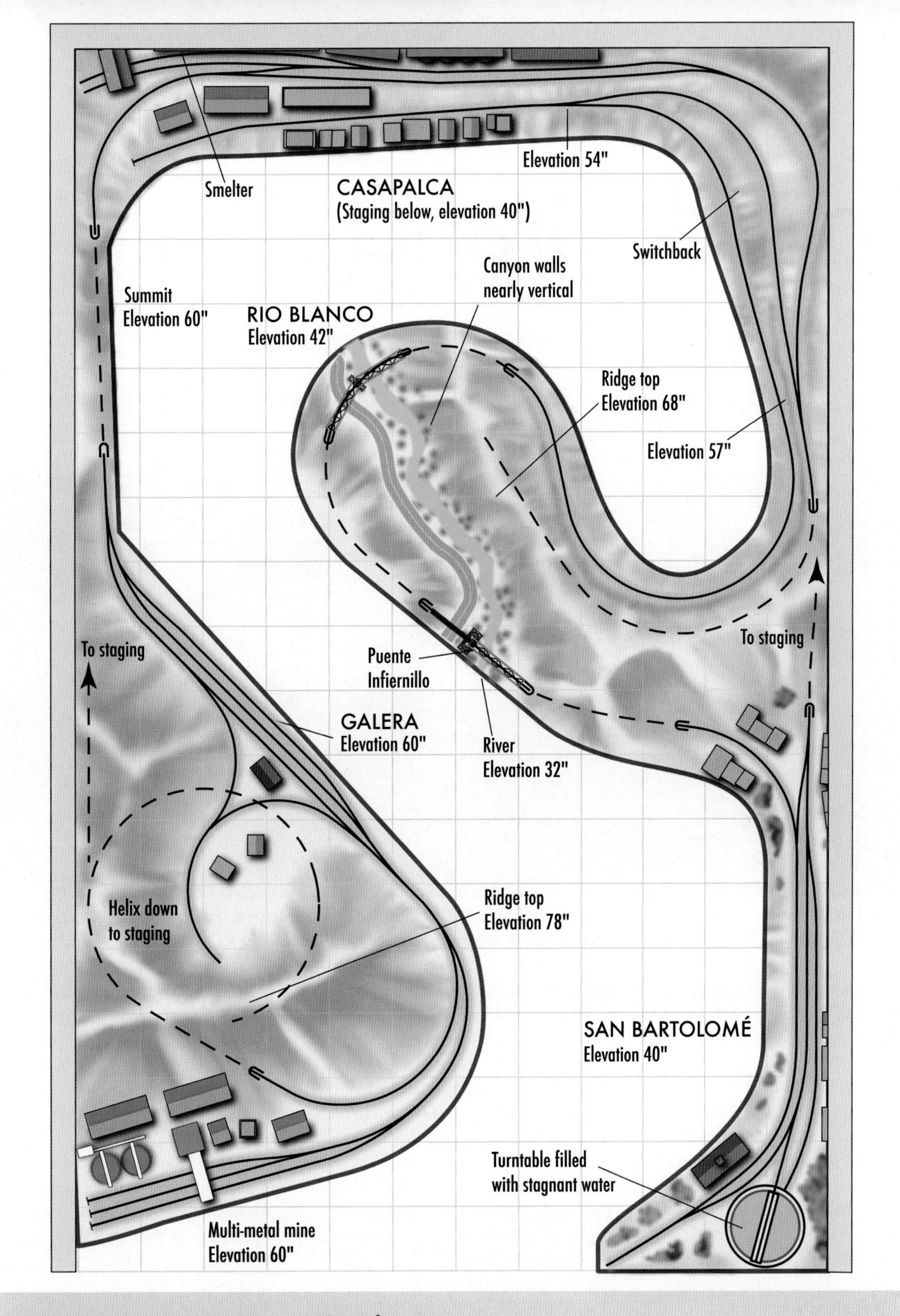

TRANS-ANDES RAILWAY — HO scale

Size: 12 x 19 feet
Prototype: FCCA
Locale: Casapalca, Peru
Era: 2015

Style: Walk-in
Mainline run: 110 feet
Minimum radius: 30" on main line, 18" on Galera wye
Turnouts: No. 6

Maximum grade: 4 percent on main line, 2.5 percent in helix
Train length: 7–8 cars

Scale of plan: ⅜" = 1 foot, 12" grid

21

Alnwick Branch

In the yard at Alnwick, a train for Alnmouth is led by a D20 class 4-4-0 locomotive. Freight cars (goods wagons) include mineral hoppers, a box van, and an oil tank wagon. *John Mallon, Aln Valley Railway Historical Society collection*

A castle, charming stone buildings, and verdant fields make Alnwick (pronounced *An-ick*) a quintessential English town. Home of Alnwick Castle (featured in the popular TV show *Downton Abbey*), the historic small town had extensive railroad facilities for passengers and freight (called *goods*).

Alnwick was located on the end of a 3-mile branch that extended west from the North Eastern Railway station at Alnmouth. The branch was double-tracked the entire way.

The layout depicts the Alnwick Branch, and a bit of the Cornhill Branch, in condensed form. Leaving staging at Alnmouth, the tracks cross a 403-foot-long stone viaduct over Cawledge Burn, a tributary of the Aln River. As the tracks round the peninsula, they pass the gasworks at the East Alnwick signal box, or control tower.

The Alnwick town scene is anchored by the exquisite Victorian stone station with twin arched vaulted sheds. The station and stone viaduct are modeled in full OO scale.

The town's extensive track arrangement is somewhat simplified. The plan uses many curved turnouts to try and capture the look of the town's smoothly flowing track. You could straighten out the tracks and use commercial track components if handlaying all the curved turnouts proves too daunting.

The design shows the Alnmouth station in visible staging, with the northern mainline tracks to Berwick veering off to the lower left. The staging tracks loosely follow the track diagram at Alnmouth, so you could build some of the structures, such as the station and engine shed, to enhance the appearance of the staging area.

This branch was incredibly busy. In the late 1920s, it saw 45 passenger trains and more than a dozen freight trains each day, including some on the Cornhill Branch. Because the area was a popular excursion destination, a wide variety of locomotives and rolling stock appeared on the Alnwick Branch. It would be a great layout for locomotive and rolling stock collectors to showcase their models.

English railroads are known for their extensive signaling. The short branch had five signal boxes and dozens of signals to control trains. Even in the simplified plan shown here, adding operational signals to this layout is a challenging task.

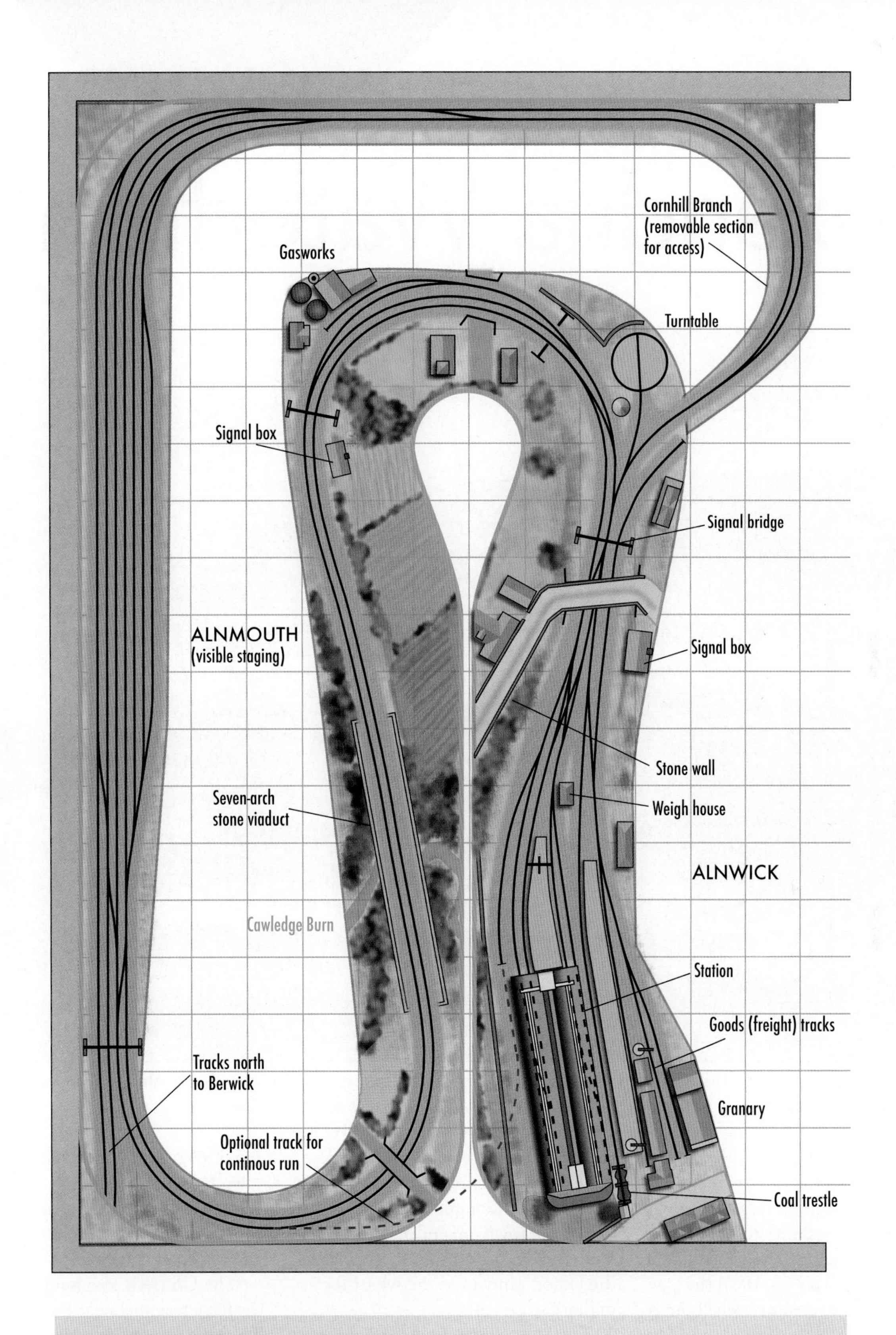

ALNWICK BRANCH — OO scale

Size: 13 x 20 feet
Prototype: London & North Eastern Railway
Locale: Alnwick, Northumberland, England

Era: 1925–1929
Style: Walk-in
Mainline run: 60 feet
Minimum radius: 18"
Turnouts: No. 6

Maximum grade: 2 percent
Train length: 10–12 cars

Scale of plan: ⅜" = 1 foot, 12" grid

22

Alexandria Waterfront

The photographer carried his camera to the top of Pioneer Mills to get this view of the Alexandria waterfront during the Civil War. *Library of Congress*

In early 1861, Alexandria, Virginia, was a busy Southern port second only to Baltimore in cargo shipping. Despite the proximity to the nation's capital, and some pro-Union sentiment in the town, on May 23, 1861, the 12,000 residents voted overwhelmingly for secession.

The next morning, Union troops invaded, and the first casualties of the war tragically occurred. Within months, the Union army transformed Alexandria into a bustling logistical supply center for Federal armies fighting in Virginia. Since most of the civilian businesses in town were not active, the military took over their facilities. For example, Pioneer Mills, one of the town's major industries, did not process and ship grain, but the Union army used the wharf for military shipments.

The Union army built a ring of forts to protect the port. On the waterfront, Battery Rodgers near the Wilkes Street Tunnel had an impressive array of heavy guns guarding the port.

The United States Military Railroad (USMRR) established a headquarters in Alexandria. It laid tracks to connect the three railroad lines that entered town to make operations more efficient. Railroad shop operations in town were expanded by adding more enginehouses and a second turntable.

The USMRR also built a railroad car ferry terminal near Battery Rodgers. This was one of the earliest railroad car ferries. It sent cars and engines to various locations on modified barges. Usually one car float a day with 8–16 cars arrived or departed from the ferry terminal.

The layout plan shows an O scale depiction of the railroad activity along

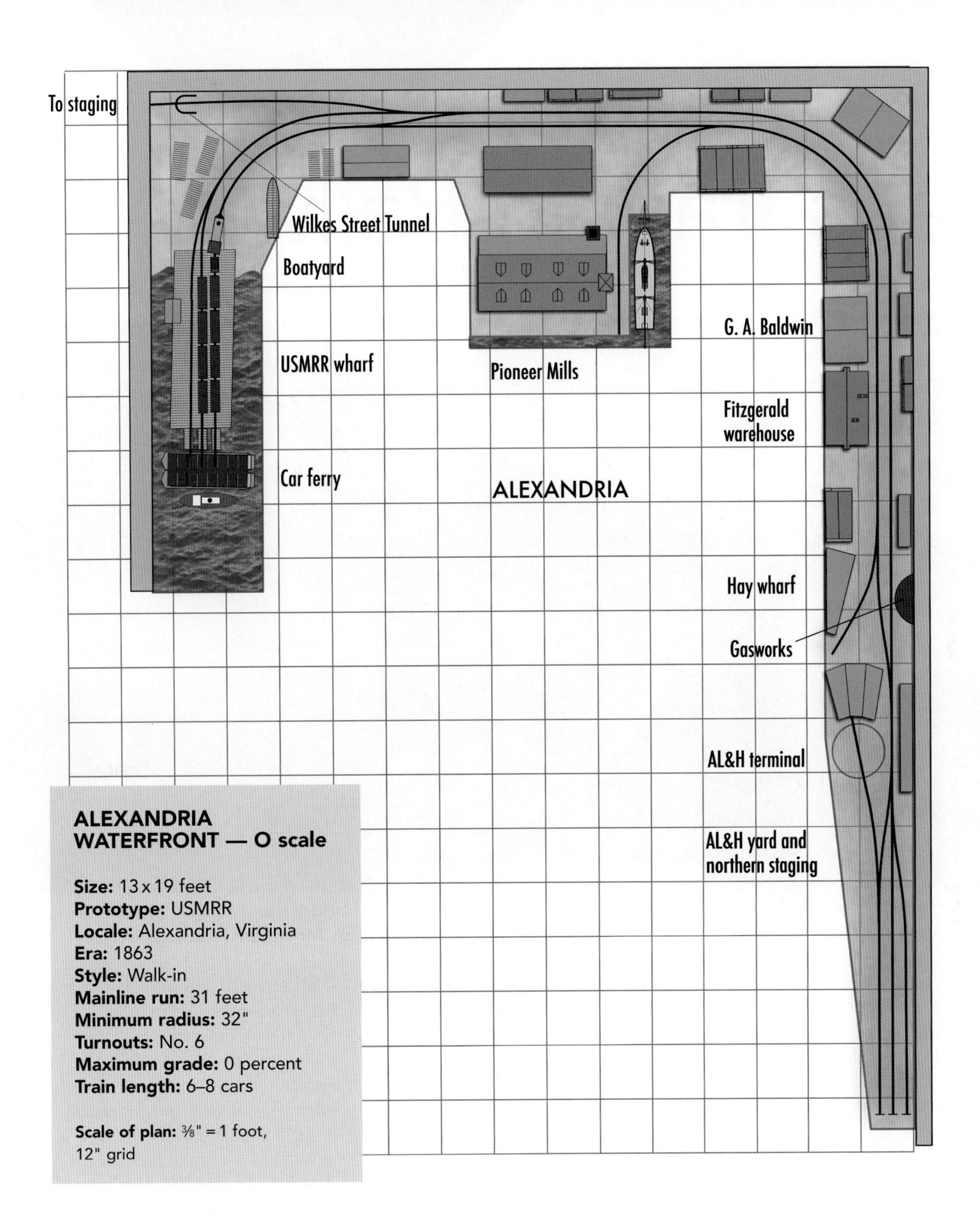

the waterfront. The plan bends the waterfront along two walls of a 13 x 19 space. The tracks on the left disappear into the Wilkes Street Tunnel. They connect to staging that would represent the Orange & Alexandria heading off to central Virginia. On the other end is the Alexandria, Loudoun & Hampshire Railroad shop facility and a visible staging yard. That staging represents the rail lines to Washington, D.C.

The car ferry at the time was arranged with lateral tracks (as opposed to longitudinal tracks), so the ferry must be moved during loading or unloading to properly position the tracks. Since moving the ferry is impractical in O scale, train operators merely pull the cars on the wharf at the start of a session. Next, they spot the outbound cars in loading order on the wharf. Since only one float a day departs, that is all that is required for a daily cycle.

The hay wharf and the mill tracks would also have cars worked in a session. A fair number of cars would move in transfer runs from southern staging at Wilkes Street to northern staging and vice versa.

Trans-Iranian Railway

A U.S. Army RSD-1 leads an inspection train across one of the thousands of bridges and toward one of the 135 tunnels on the Amercian-run portion of the Trans-Iranian Railway in the Zagros Mountains. *National Archives*

From the Persian Gulf to the Caspian Sea, the Trans-Iranian Railway crosses some of the world's most difficult terrain.

When WWII erupted, Russia and Great Britain jointly invaded Iran to secure the railroad for resupplying Russia. The United States Military Railway Service (USMRS) arrived in 1942 and took over operation of the line from the Persian Gulf to Teheran. The double-deck layout depicts the line from Bandar Shahpur to Dorud in a point-to-point design.

The port at Bandar Shahpur, with a small Y-shaped wharf, was inadequate, so the British built a port at Khorramshahr and linked it with a new 75-mile branch line. The layout depicts half the Bandar Shahpur wharf, while Khorramshahr is modeled by lower level staging.

Leaving Bandar Shahpur, the layout's tracks proceed directly to Andimeshk, the railroad's division point. Here, trains get a second engine on the point. This is also where the layout's branch from Khorramshahr connects.

Then the line enters the Zagros Mountains, a region with bleak ravines between sheer and desolate peaks. The prototype line climbs high in the mountains and plunges through tunnel after tunnel—135 of them in one stretch of 165 miles. The layout includes eight tunnels and six bridges.

The yard at Dorud functions as an active, visible staging yard. A model train crew terminates here by cutting off the engines and positioning them on the opposite end. The train is then ready for a new crew to make the return run. Open-top cars have their loads removed and readied for use on the next northbound train.

You will find a wide variety of rolling stock on the line. Most original Iranian rolling stock was of German origin. The British and Americans brought equipment of their own design as well as French and Indian cars. American locomotives were primarily USATC S200 2-8-2s and RSD-1s. Neither are readily available in HO scale, but you could modify USRA light Mikados or an Alco RSD-3 to resemble those engines. Davenport 0-4-0s, British 2-8-0s in OO scale, German 2-10-0s and 2-8-0s in HO, and even a few Garratt 2-8-4+4-8-2 articulated locomotives could be used. Almost all the locomotives were oil-burners.

The railcars should have European-style links and buffers.

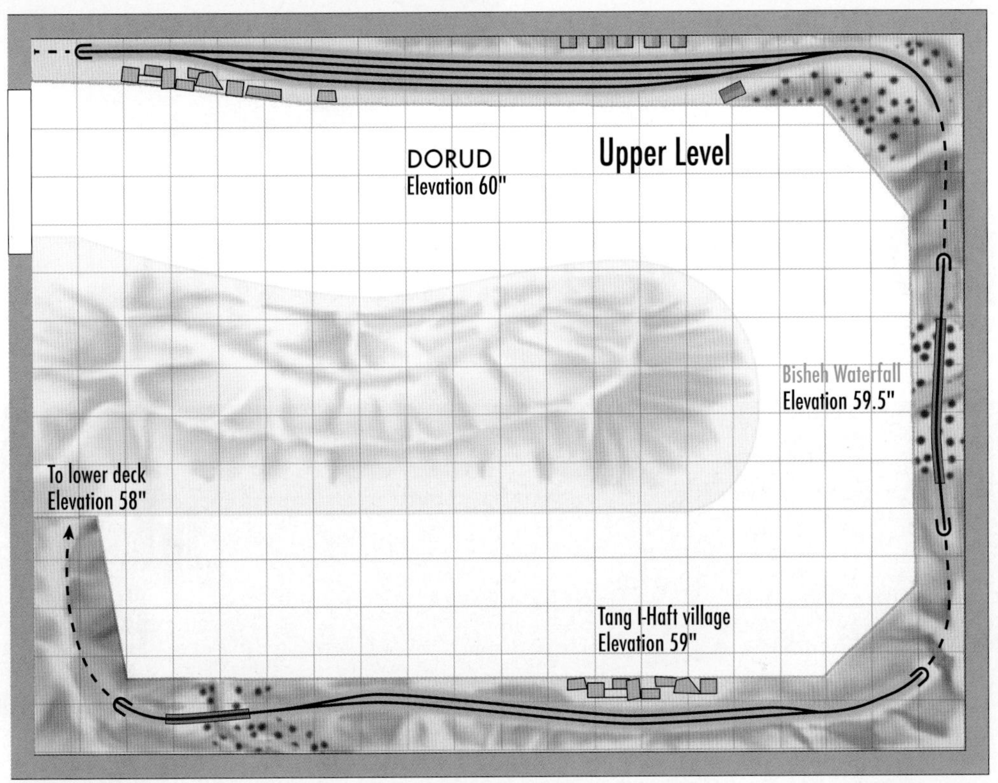

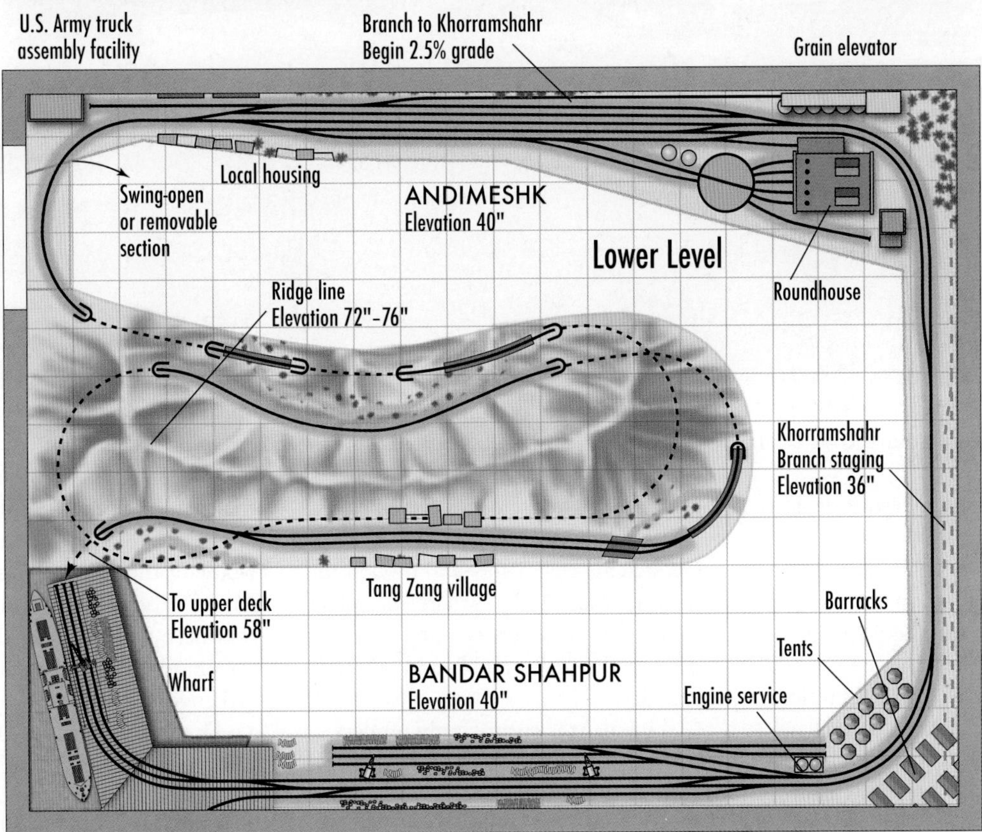

TRANS-IRANIAN RAILWAY — HO scale

Size: 15 x 20 feet
Prototype: United States Military Railway Service
Locale: Bandar Shahpur, Iran
Era: Late 1944

Style: Multideck, walk-in
Mainline run: 220 feet
Minimum radius: 24" main line
Turnouts: No. 6

Maximum grade: 3 percent
Train length: 15 cars

Scale of plan: ¼" = 1 foot, 12" grid

24

EMD Progress Rail

Four of Norfolk Southern's SD70 heritage units pose in front of the Progress Rail EMD locomotive factory in Muncie, Indiana, a scene that could be replicated on this layout. *Casey Thomason, Norfolk Southern*

This room-size layout depicts the Electro-Motive Diesel (EMD) Progress Rail Services (PRS) locomotive factory in Muncie, Indiana. The layout also includes a local branch line with rail-served battery and plastics factories.

PRS, a subsidiary of Caterpillar Inc., bought EMD in 2011. PRS closed EMD's locomotive assembly plant in London, Ontario, and then opened the locomotive assembly plant in Muncie. EMD's headquarters and engineering group remained in La Grange, Illinois. The Muncie plant joins a long list of rail-related factories and repair facilities run by PRS throughout the world.

The original building was built in 1961 by Westinghouse, and workers there produced large power transformers until 1998. The factory was well suited for heavy locomotive production. PRS invested approximately $50 million to renovate the 740,000 square-foot plant, completing the conversion by adding state-of-the-art assembly and painting facilities.

The plant is surprisingly modest, considering the size of the objects it produces. Nonetheless, the layout only depicts half of the main T-shaped structure and spurs.

The central bay of the building is where the final assembly takes place. The spur behind the assembly building is the track to the paint shop. Incoming materials and parts go to the two spurs to the right of the central bay.

The main factory building and a tree line help hide two staging tracks that depict Norfolk Southern's former Nickel Plate New Castle Subdivision. Many of the locomotives built at Muncie travel out as loads on Norfolk Southern, either on flatcars, if they are not standard gauge, or pulled behind NS engines.

The layout includes an oval test track, which is an unusual, but prototypically correct, feature of the layout.

The rest of the branch provides a bit of switching variety as the plastics and battery factories can take an assortment of cars.

The surrounding terrain is relatively flat, and the site partially borders a golf course. With a constant parade of new engines to look at, railfans are likely to be very distracted when playing the course.

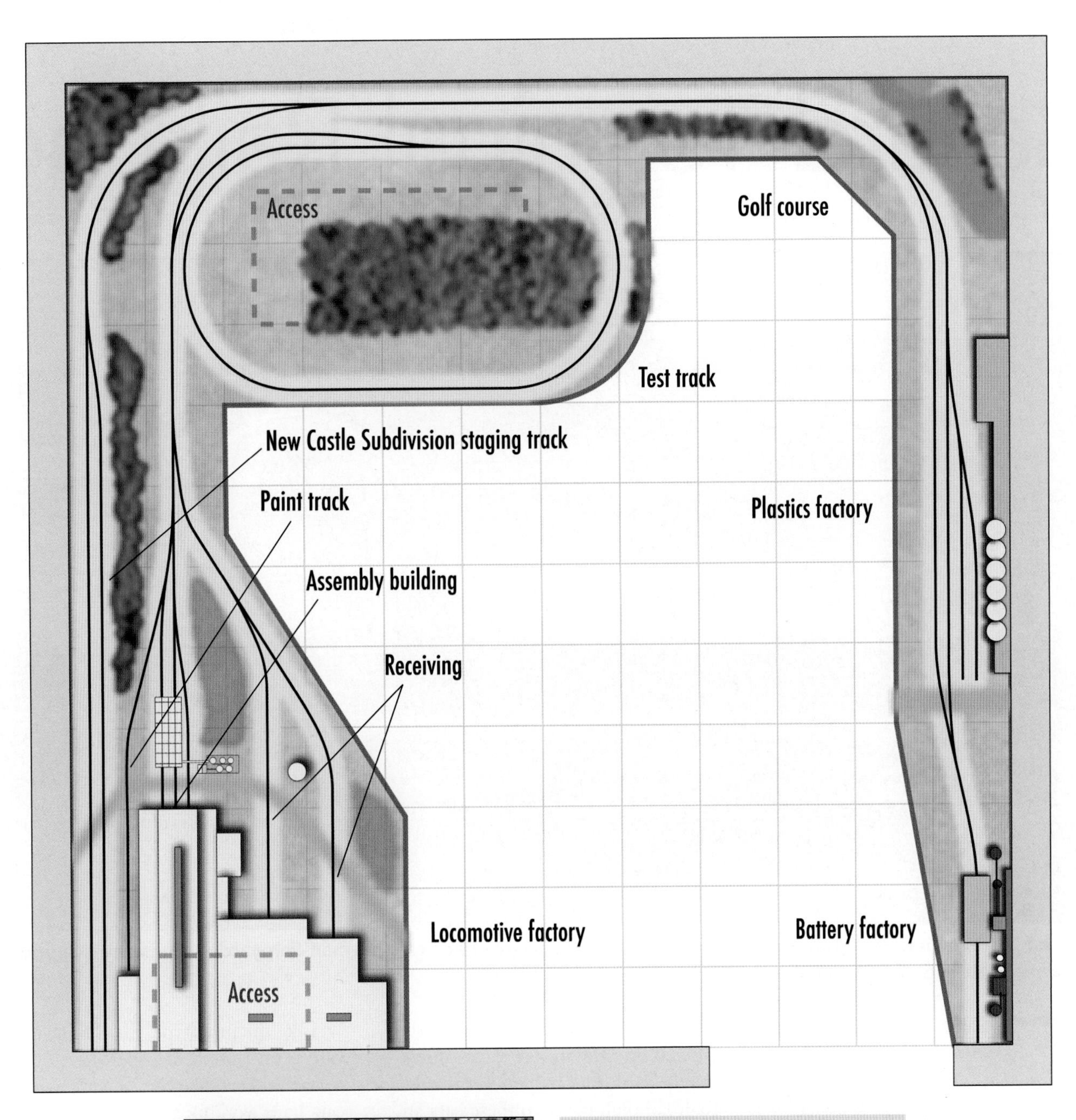

Locomotives for export sit on the main assembly line. *Progress Rail*

EMD PROGRESS RAIL — HO scale

Size: 12 x 12 feet
Prototype: Norfolk Southern
Locale: Muncie, Indiana
Era: 2015
Style: Walk-in
Mainline run: 36 feet
Minimum radius: 22"
Turnouts: No. 6
Maximum grade: 0 percent
Train length: 10 cars

Scale of plan: ½" = 1 foot, 12" grid

25

Ballard Terminal Railroad

Ballard Terminal no. 98, a former Milwaukee Road SW1, passes Pacific Fisherman Shipyard, a signature scene on this small railroad. *Ben Bachman*

The Ballard Terminal Railroad is a 3-mile-long short line that runs on the north side of Salmon Bay in the Ballard area of Seattle. It runs on a former Great Northern branch line. In service since 1893, the branch has served numerous industries in the waterfront area.

In 1997, BNSF, GN's successor, decided to abandon the branch due to declining business. Three of the remaining rail-served customers then formed the Ballard Terminal Railroad. That number has now dwindled to one business, the Salmon Bay Sand & Gravel Co., but some new business may develop in the future.

A transfer run from BNSF's Interbay Yard delivers 4–6 carloads of cement, fly ash, stucco, and mortar ordered by Salmon Bay to the interchange yard. The Ballard Terminal Railroad then picks up these cars and delivers them to Salmon Bay. The layout includes a section of the BNSF line that allows the transfer run to be actively modeled.

The track plan follows the prototype fairly closely with some selective compression. It includes additional spurs used by customers other than the sand and gravel plant for added operational interest.

If you wanted more switching activity, the layout could be backdated to when the branch was busier by making the abandoned tracks active and serving industries.

Like the prototype, the interchange yard is on a grade. Cars left here need to have their brakes set. Since few HO cars have working brakes, a chock or pin could be used to hold the cars.

The Ballard Terminal Railroad has one switcher in service, an ex-Milwaukee Road SW1. The engine, no. 98, sports a neat red and gray livery and is nicknamed *Li'l Beaver* in honor of a local school. The railroad has two other engines in storage, but they are not operational.

The streets and industries should be populated with numerous cars, trucks, and small boats. The backdrop should depict the nearby Salmon Bay, which is just behind the buildings on three sides of the layout.

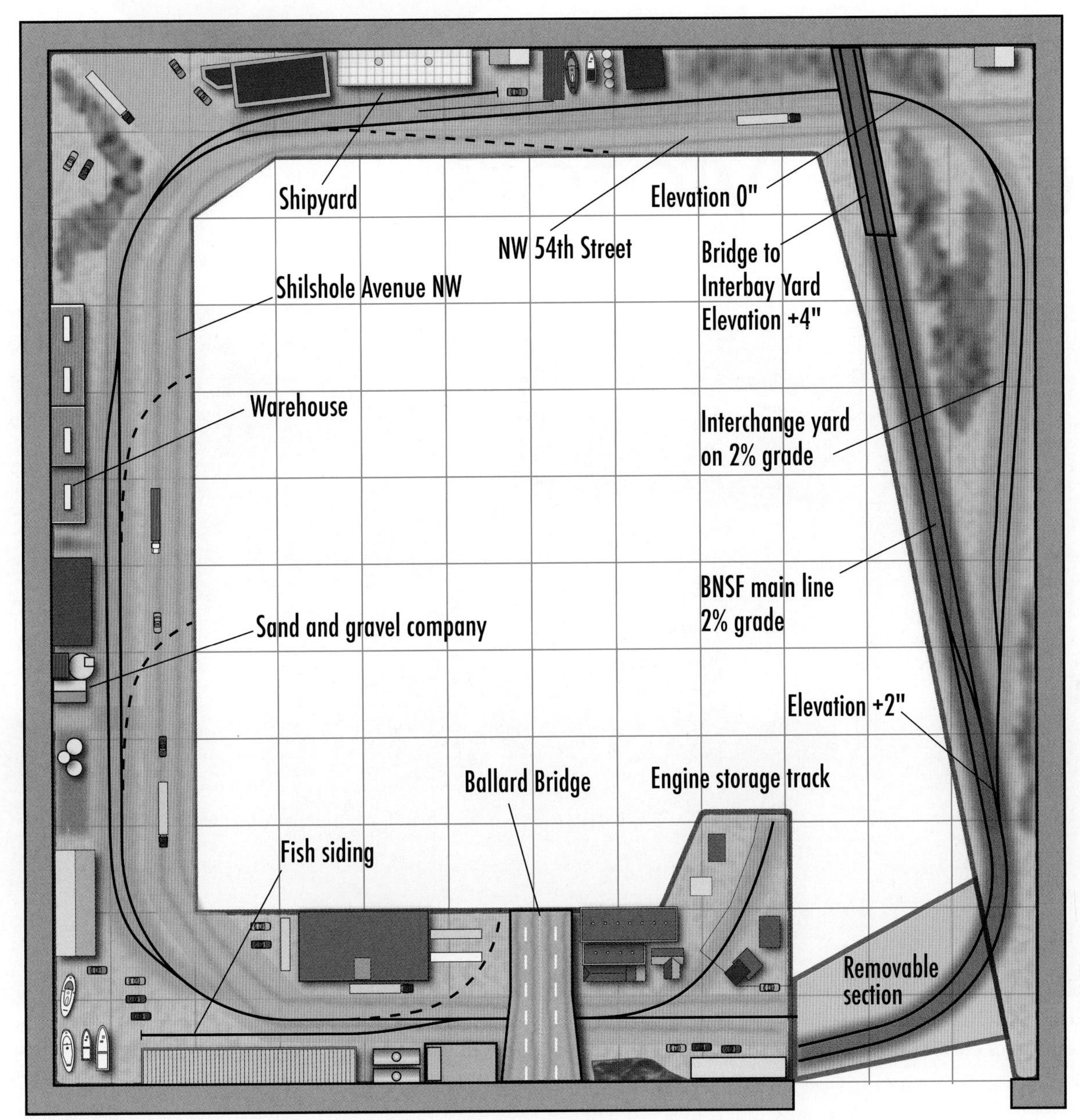

Dotted black lines are abandoned tracks that can be used if backdating the layout to GN era.

Salmon Bay Sand & Gravel is the last customer using rail service on the line, but the branch was much busier in the past. The layout could easily be set in that era.

BALLARD TERMINAL RAILROAD — HO scale

Size: 12 x 12 feet
Prototype: Ballard Terminal, BNSF
Locale: Seattle, Washington
Era: 2008
Style: Walk-in
Mainline run: 36 feet
Minimum radius: 24"
Turnouts: No. 6
Maximum grade: 2 percent
Train length: 4–6 cars

Scale of plan: ½" = 1 foot, 12" grid

Sunon Motors

Canadian National brings a train down the former GTW main line south of Detroit. The train has a load of auto racks and cars carrying auto parts in tow that would be typical of the cars switched on this layout.

It is somewhat ironic that the automobile industry relies extensively on railroads for shipping parts as well as completed autos and trucks.

This layout depicts a freelanced automobile assembly plant located in southern Michigan in the current era. The plant is owned by Sunon (a notional company), and it assembles small sport utility vehicles. I based the operating scheme on a composite of several automobile assembly plants in the United States.

Two railroads serve this plant, the Canadian National, via a former Grand Trunk Western line, and Norfolk Southern, via an former Conrail line. However, only the CN actually spots cars in the plant, and only CN engines are needed to run the layout.

The CN and NS yards serve as visible staging yards. An operating session begins with cars on these tracks billed to spots in the Sunon plant or at a shingle factory. Two CN crews could work the layout. One switches the CN yard, and the other works the cars in the NS yard. There is an access hole to allow a better reach of the CN yard. The transfer runs from the yards to the respective railroad main lines, which are not included in this layout. However, the train crews set up the trains for departure.

Three railroad spurs serve the plant. The central spur gets tank cars loaded with oil products. The other two spurs actually enter the main assembly building. The railroad brings cars loaded with parts to those two spurs. The cars must be spotted in precise locations. However, these tracks can only be actively switched during 30-minute shift changes at the plant.

Therefore, both CN train crews need to sort and pre-block the cars for these spurs in the correct sequence, so they can be switched in the short time frame available. The crews have to plan ahead and be ready to go when the whistle blows for shift change.

Modern automobile assembly plants are usually very large, flat buildings. Some can be nearly a mile long. They have few windows, but the roofs feature a variety of stacks and ventilators, especially over the paint shop.

Even at 8 feet long and 4 feet wide, the modeled portion of this plant is

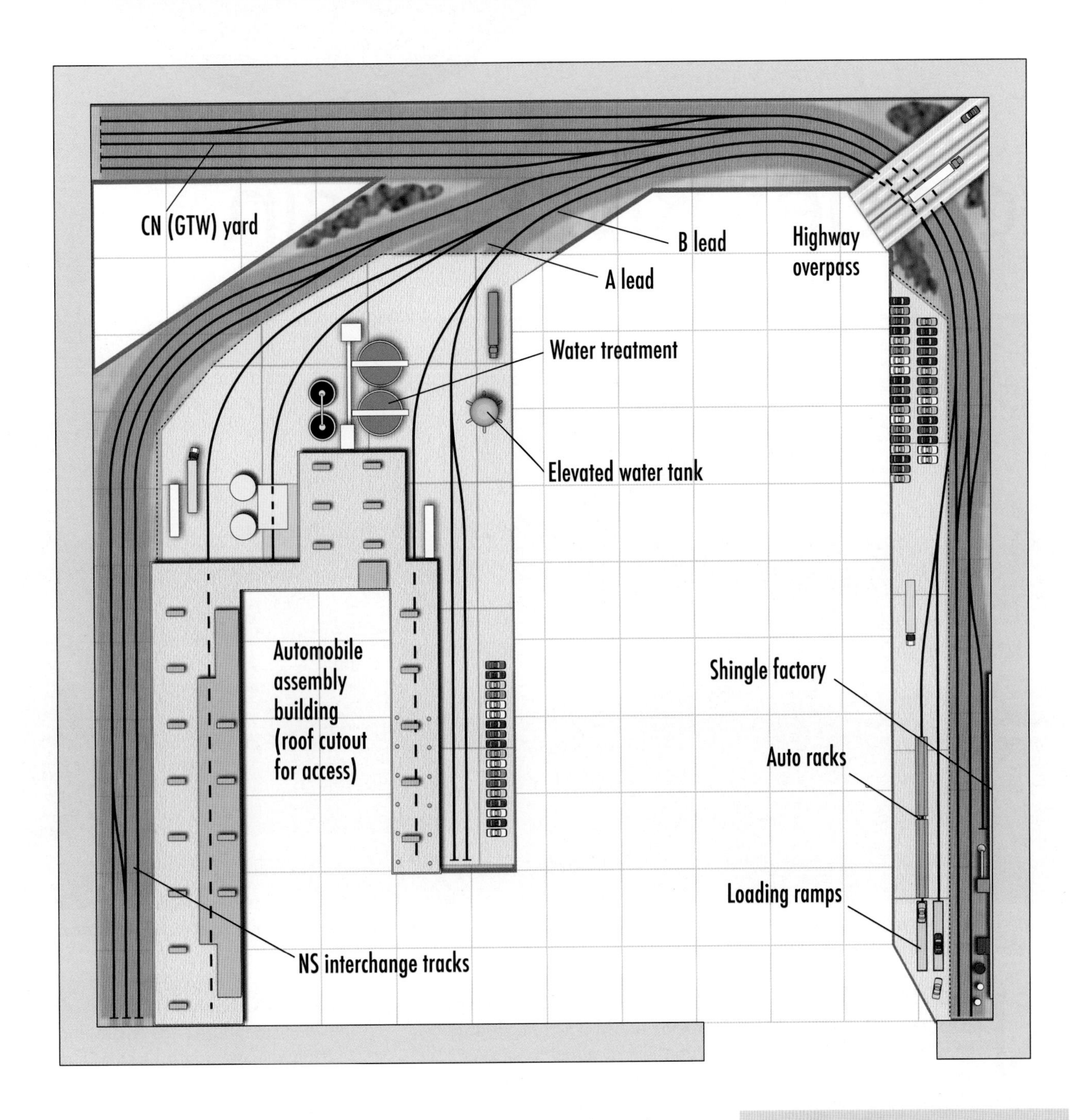

selectively compressed, but it captures the large area that these building occupy. The assembly plant on the layout has a U shape, and the center section is cut out to allow access to the internal tracks. A removable roof could be added to cover the center of the plant when taking photos or when the train operators do not need access. The open interior provides an opportunity for lots of detailing and lighting.

The water tank is a prominent scenic feature that lends some vertical relief to this otherwise fairly flat scene. It should proudly display the company's name.

The right side of the layout houses the auto-rack loading ramps for the plant. The stub tracks can hold five auto racks at a time. These tracks can be switched when convenient.

This side of the layout also has a shingle factory served by a single spur. This factory receives covered hoppers with roofing granules and tank cars with tar and other chemicals.

Most of the terrain around the plant is paved with concrete. The corner with the highway bridge has some vegetation. Since the plant is in a suburban area, photo backdrops could be used to depict the surrounding countryside.

SUNON MOTORS — HO scale

Size: 12 x 12 feet
Prototype: Freelanced
Locale: Southern Michigan
Era: 2015
Style: Walk-in
Mainline run: 36 feet
Minimum radius: 30"
Turnouts: No. 6
Maximum grade: 0 percent
Train length: 6 cars

Scale of plan: ½" = 1 foot, 12" grid

27

Powder River Basin

Trains run in every direction at Nacco Junction in this 2008 scene. This is the kind of heavy coal-hauling action that the layout features. *Matt Van Hattem*

No other coal deposit on the planet is so big, so close to the surface, and so cheap to mine as the rich seams found in eastern Wyoming and southern Montana. The railroading needed to haul this coal to market is on a scale unseen anywhere else. More than 100 trains a day from two railroads serve the multiple-track BNSF Orin Subdivision, which includes some portions jointly owned by the Union Pacific.

The layout is a room-sized N scale depiction of the northern end of the Orin Line. However, with minor modifications in track spacing, it could also be built in Z scale. Because of space constraints, the layout is not an exact copy of the prototype, but it creates an impression of the Orin Line by capturing the line's look and operation.

The plan uses multiple loops to provide nonstop action. Continuous action is well suited to smaller scale layouts on which long coal trains, 30 cars in N or 40 cars in Z scale, are the main show. It is not unusual for trains to meet or overtake one another on the Orin Line, and this plan supports that type of operation.

The bent dogbone (oval) plan uses a three-track line with junctions at each end of the dogbone. Coal Creek Junction leads to the Coal Creek Mine. It has two sidings capable of staging a design-length train. These could be loaded at the start of an operating session, and they would be replaced by empties during the session. Thus, you need not worry about loading and emptying hoppers during an operating session.

Donkey Creek Junction represents the connection to BNSF's main line to Montana and South Dakota. The BNSF main line makes an oval around the perimeter of the room to allow trains other than unit coal to run on the layout. There is a power plant here, but it is not rail served. The coal it burns is mined on site and delivered by conveyor.

But the Orin Line is more than a coal hauler. In the 21st century, gas and oil are also being extracted from this area. The sidings at the Hilight gas plant provide rail service to the 1,056-mile Hilight natural gas gathering system. This system supplies low- and high-pressure gas extracted from the area to the Hilight plant for processing. The Hilight system has a capacity of approximately 30 million cubic feet per day and utilizes refrigeration to process

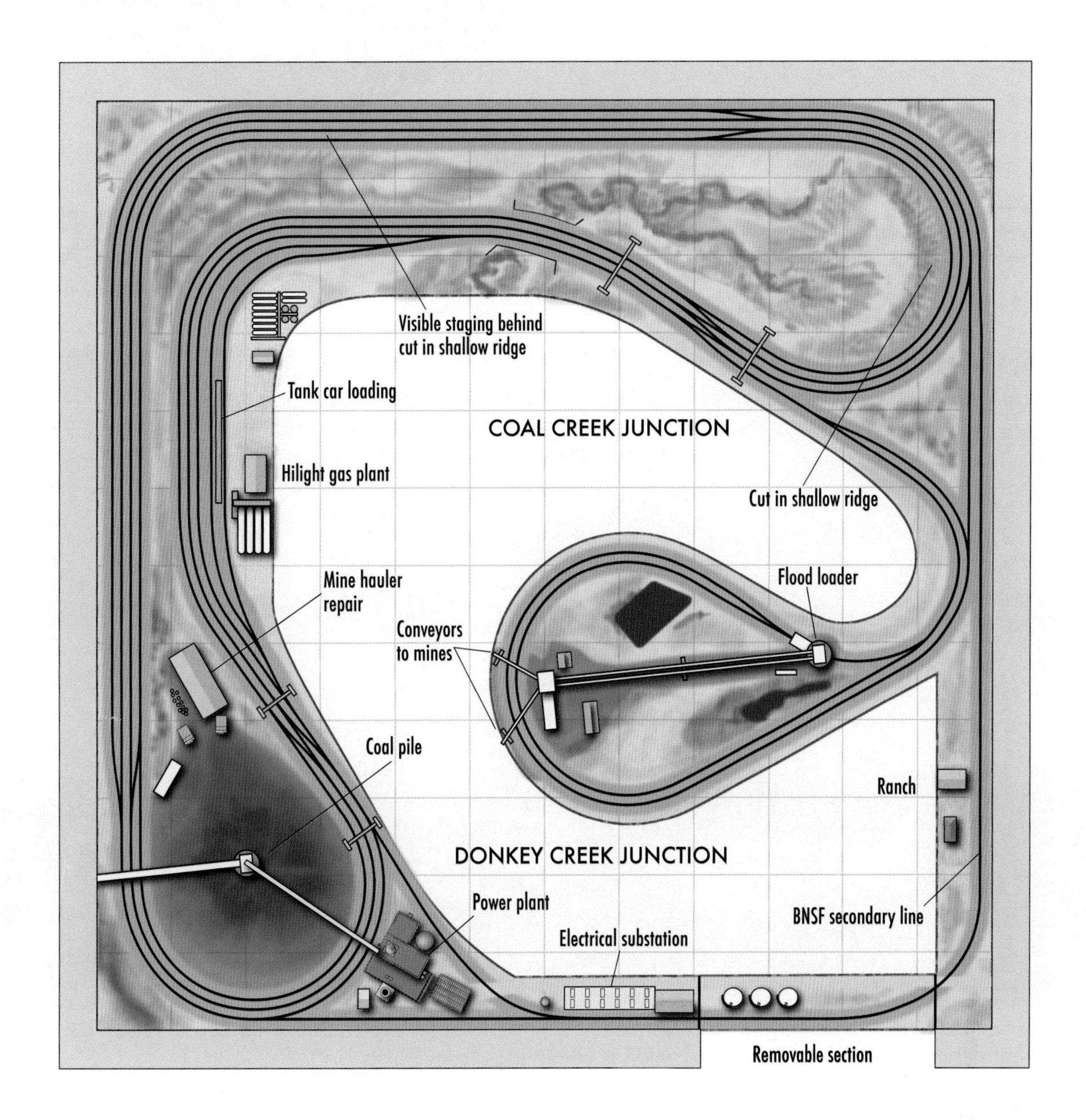

propane, butane, and natural gasoline. Some is shipped by rail in tank cars, and the rest by pipeline. This is the only industry on the layout that doesn't utilize unit trains. Tank cars get spotted here as in traditional railroad operations.

Along the back is a visible, four-track staging yard. In some places, the tracks are partially obscured by cuts in shallow ridges. Mounting the layout at near eye level helps disguise the tracks in the cuts. You could add helices at each loop to drop the staging tracks below the layout. That would provide space for more staging tracks at the expense of additional layout complexity.

The scenery in this location is deceptively simple with wind-swept, grass-covered rolling hills. Grass, small shrubs, and trees should cover areas that man has not disturbed. The creekbed, in particular, should be covered with green vegetation. You can use satellite photos available online to get an idea of the surprising variety of colors and textures that comprise this region.

The terrain is mostly open with numerous hills and ridges. The layout takes advantage of the shallow hills to create cuts at the dogbone ends to help hide the turn-back curves. However, they need not be fully hidden, as this area is rife with coal loops and 180 degree curves. Seeing tracks in the distance loaded with cars is not unusual.

Numerous industrial structures along the railroad will keep you busy modeling a variety of buildings.

POWDER RIVER BASIN — N or Z scale

Size: 12 x 12 feet
Prototype: UP, BNSF
Locale: Donkey Creek Junction, Wyoming
Era: 2015
Style: Walk-in
Mainline run: 48 feet
Minimum radius: 18"
Turnouts: No. 6
Maximum grade: 0 percent
Train length: 30–40 cars

Scale of plan: ½" = 1 foot, 12" grid

28

DaniCa Forest Products

The paper mill at West Point, Virginia, serves as a prototype for this layout. Bulkhead flatcars carry cut pulp logs that are unloaded in the flume. The crane unloads whole logs from trucks.

Even today, a paper mill makes a good subject for a model railroad. Railroads use a variety of car types to service a paper mill including bulkhead flatcars, tank cars, open wood-chip gondolas, covered hoppers, coal hoppers, and boxcars.

DaniCa Forest Products is a free-lanced chemical process paper mill typically found in the Southeast. (The *Ca* represents its Canadian owners.) In addition to making paper pulp, the chemical process creates various chemical by-products including that funky paper mill smell. Most by-products are recycled or shipped out as commodities.

As depicted on the layout, the mill can accept pulp logs on bulkhead flatcars, or wood chips on tractor trailers. A specialized unloader that looks like a backhoe mounted on a rail gantry knocks the pulp logs into a water flume. The flume then transports the logs to a drum debarker and chipper.

Fresh chips join others brought in by truck on a wood-chip pile. An array of conveyors moves the chips from the piles to the kraft mill, where they get converted to pulp. The pulp is shipped out as an intermediate product, but much of it moves to the Fourdrinier machine house, where it is made into paper.

Most buildings come from Walthers kits, although some need to be kitbashed to make them longer and narrower. Scratchbuilding is necessary for the conveyors and log and chip unloaders.

The detailed structures provide a modeling challenge. With tall buildings on each side of the tracks and conveyors crossing overhead, the layout offers an industrial canyon for visual spectacle.

DANICA FOREST PRODUCTS — HO scale

Size: 12 x 18 feet
Prototype: Norfolk Southern
Locale: Southeast United States
Era: 2001
Style: Walk-in
Mainline run: 46 feet
Minimum radius: 30"
Turnouts: No. 6
Maximum grade: 0 percent
Train length: 10–12 cars

Scale of plan: 3/8" = 1 foot, 12" grid

The interchange yard has room for other industries. The plan has a veneer factory but any industry would do.

If space allows, this layout could be expanded as shown on the plan.

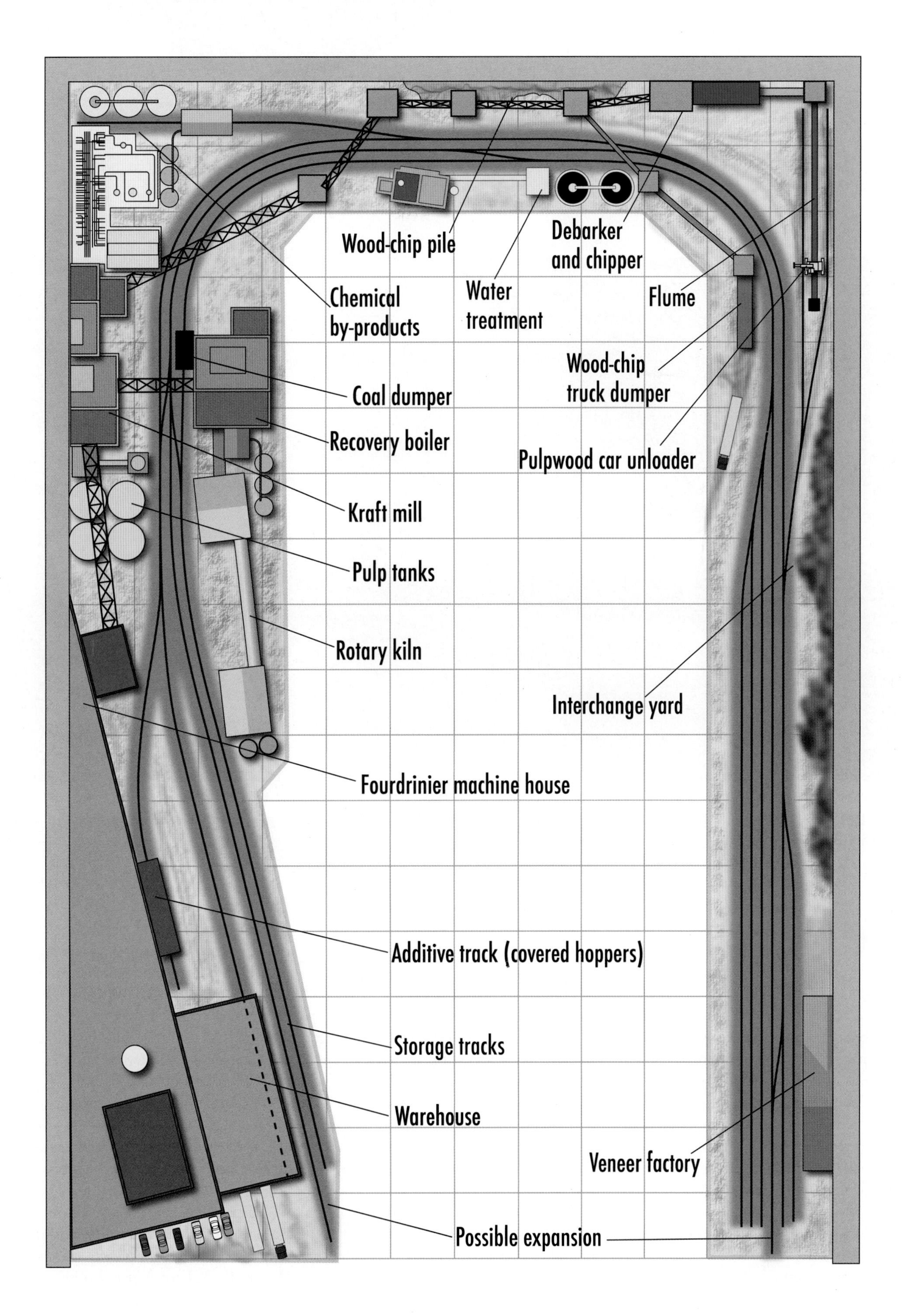
Wood-chip pile
Debarker and chipper
Chemical by-products
Water treatment
Flume
Wood-chip truck dumper
Coal dumper
Recovery boiler
Pulpwood car unloader
Kraft mill
Pulp tanks
Rotary kiln
Interchange yard
Fourdrinier machine house
Additive track (covered hoppers)
Storage tracks
Warehouse
Veneer factory
Possible expansion

Rockport & Weak

A three-story building in O scale makes an effective view block as illustrated by this New England mill scene at the turn of the 19th century. The cars shown are standard gauge, while narrow gauge cars would be smaller. *Library of Congress*

Maine's two-foot railroads are an intriguing but sometimes difficult subject for narrow gauge modelers. However, by using On30 equipment, a smooth-running railroad can be built with a reasonable expenditure on rolling stock and track. Modelers willing to accept the gauge discrepancy have many options of ready-to-run models.

This freelanced plan depicts a short Maine narrow gauge line in On30 scale. It shows a railroad that brings stone, lumber, and finished mill products from the Maine hinterland to be shipped at Rockport, a small seaport.

Rockport represents a typical small Maine port. It features finger wharves for shipping granite, lumber, crops, and finished goods. The trains bring coal and general cargo back to the countryside from the port.

On the plan, the ship shown at the dock is a typical Maine lumber schooner. No kits exist for such a ship, so it would have to be scratchbuilt.

The area between the wharves is left open to allow access to the tracks.

After leaving Rockport, the line passes over a low wood trestle and crosses a branch of the standard gauge Maine Central Railroad. A ball signal controls this intersection, even though the standard gauge line is a dummy.

Next, the railroad approaches Weak. This is the junction of two branches that go off to staging behind the mill.

The town of Weak was inspired by an Iain Rice design based on Strong, Maine (similar to his Sheepscot plan that appeared in *Model Railroad Planning 2009*). I modified the track plan to make it a sectional layout. I omitted the integral curved backdrop and used a mill building as a view block of the fiddle area. This makes the layout portable and viewable from front and back.

The three sections that comprise Weak could be taken out of the layout and displayed at shows either standalone or as part of a larger sectional layout.

(Plan 32 on pages 68–69 shows a large On30 layout that is based more closely on the narrow gauge Wiscasset, Waterville & Farmington Railway.)

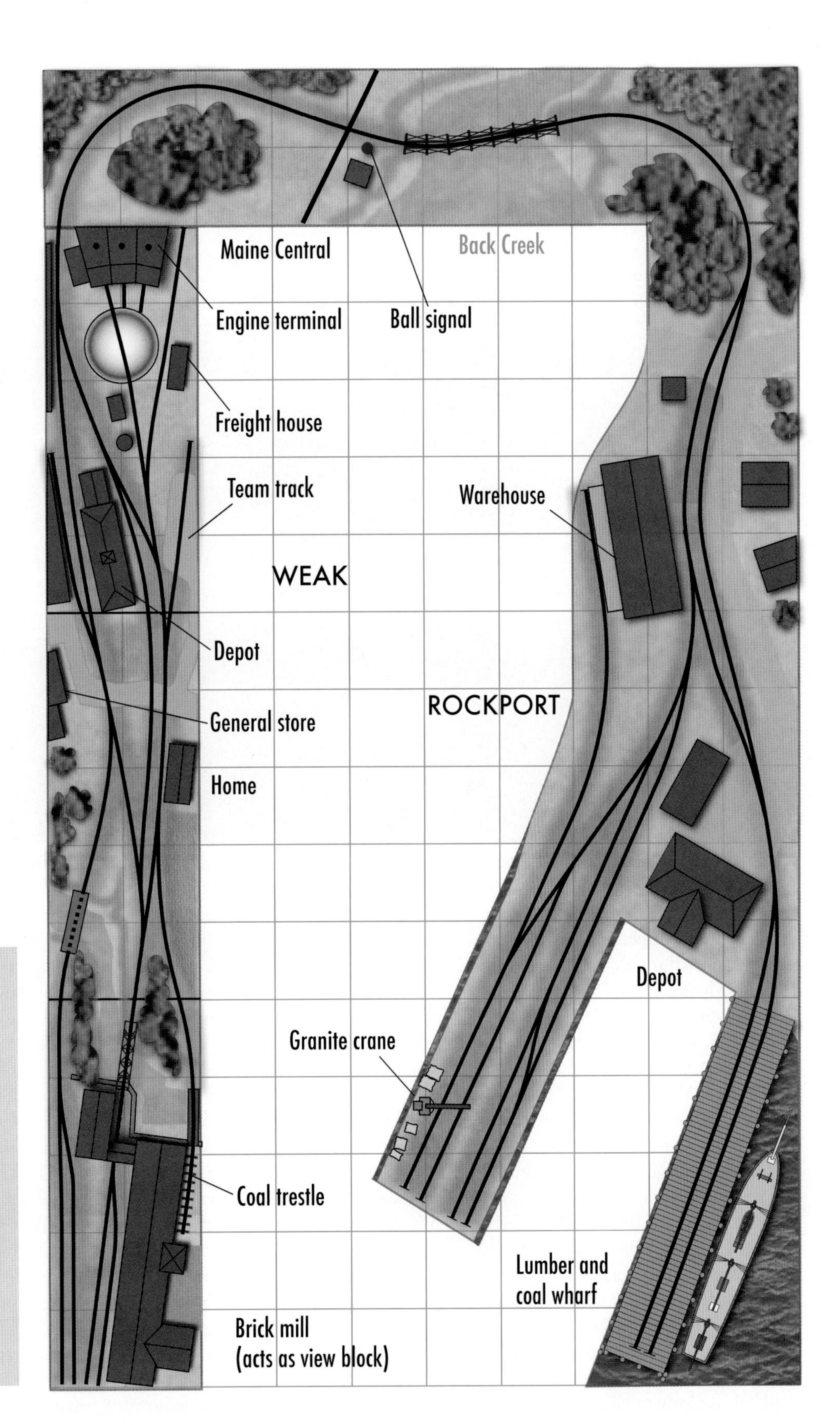

ROCKPORT & WEAK — On30 scale

Size: 10 x 15 feet
Prototype: Freelanced
Locale: Rockport, Maine
Era: 1932
Style: Walk-in
Mainline run: 38 feet
Minimum radius: 0"
Turnouts: No. 6
Maximum grade: 0 percent
Train length: 6–8 cars

Scale of plan:
½" = 1 foot, 12" grid

Soldier Summit

Three BNSF General Electric diesels lead a manifest freight westbound approaching Colton, Utah, in April 2002.

The Utah & Pleasant Valley Railway opened a narrow gauge route through the Wasatch Mountains in 1878, which crested at Soldier Summit. (Named for several U.S. Army soldiers who perished there during a freak blizzard in July 1861. The soldiers were Southerners given permission to leave Camp Floyd and join the Confederate army.)

This is Utah's highest (7,440 feet) and steepest main line. Descending to the west, the grade tilted to more than 4 percent before following the Spanish Fork River to Provo and then to Salt Lake City. The Denver & Rio Grande Western bought the U&PV in 1882 and converted it to standard gauge in 1890.

In 1913, the D&RGW agreed with the Utah Railway to jointly operate the line. The railroads improved the route by reducing the western slope to 2 percent.

In 1981, the D&RGW bought the Southern Pacific and took on its name. Then in 1996, the UP and SP merged. To improve competition, the ICC granted the Burlington Northern Santa Fe Railway trackage rights over the former D&RGW main line. The BNSF contracted with Utah Railway to operate its coal and local trains.

This double-deck, N scale layout fits a long, narrow space. The era is in the early 21st century when the coal mine at Willow Creek was still active.

A westbound train comes out of the staging helix and heads across relatively flat land until it reaches Helper. The town is aptly named, because here the railroad adds helper engines for the climb to Soldier Summit.

The staging helix is a rounded oval. It has two loops with four tracks at a 1.8 percent grade. Each loop is about 21 feet long, so there are about 168 feet of track in the helix—more than enough to stage eight 12-foot-long trains. Several crossovers in the helix allow trains to be staged and run in a random sequence.

The plan features two coal mines and the Sunnyvale coal branch. A power plant next to the Willow Creek Mine burns coal that is mined on site.

The Utah Railway enters the main line from its staging at Utah Railway Junction next to the power plant.

The top deck mostly runs through empty desert across the summit, Gilluly Loops, and into the Thistle Tunnels.

The Thistle Tunnels are perhaps the newest railway tunnels in the United States. They were built in response to a massive landslide in 1983 that dammed the river that was flooding the town of Thistle and the D&RGW's small yard.

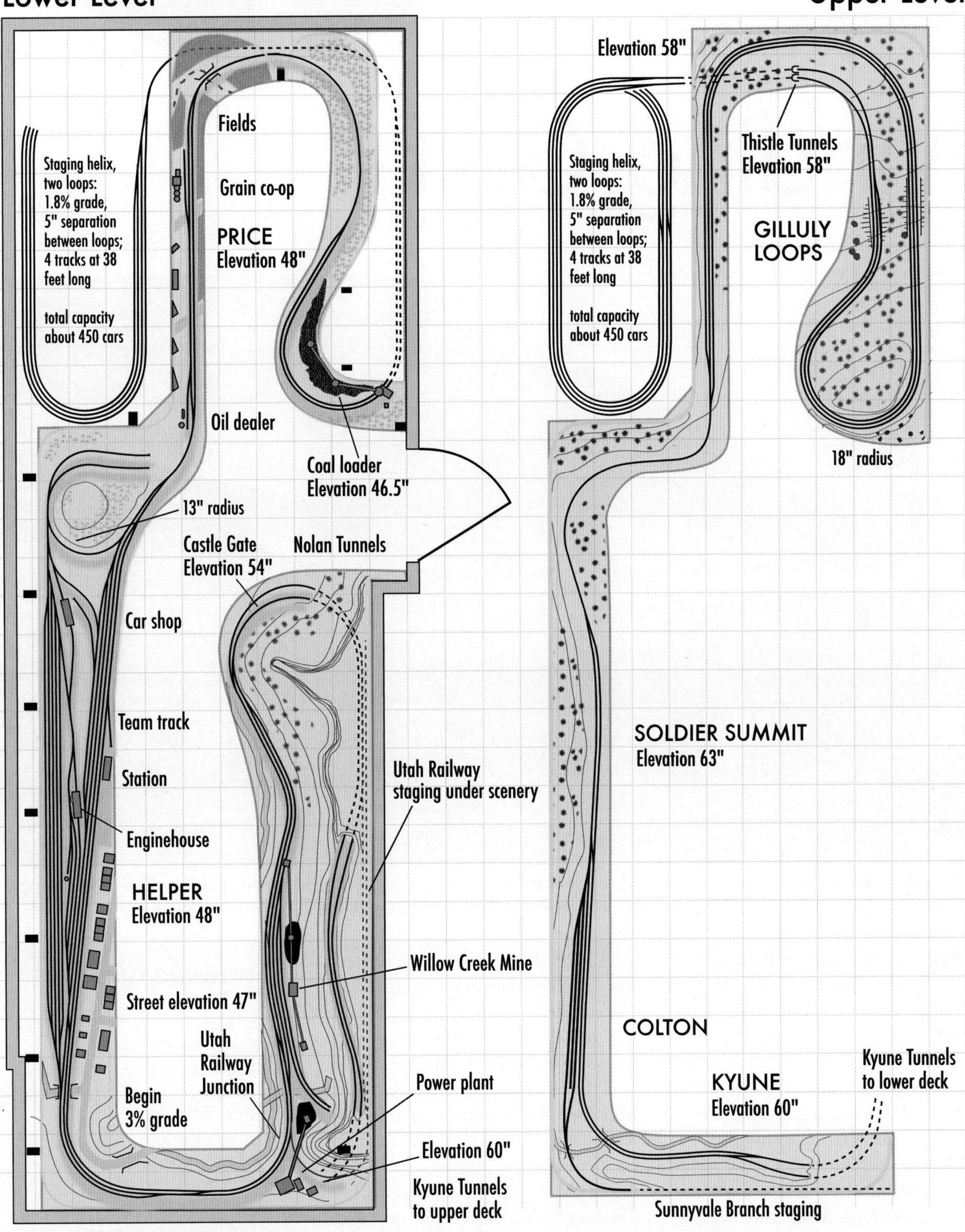

SOLDIER SUMMIT — N scale

Size: 10 x 30 feet
Prototype: UP, BNSF, Utah Railway
Locale: Soldier Summit, Utah
Era: 2000–2010

Style: Multideck, walk-in
Mainline run: 220 feet
Minimum radius: 18" main line, 13" in the wye
Turnouts: No. 6

Maximum grade: 3 percent
Train length: 30 cars

Scale of plan: ¼" = 1 foot, 12" grid

31

Winding Gulf

Lillybrook Coal Co. Mine No. 3 on the Stonecoal Branch was a typical tipple in this region. The C&O hoppers were probably spotted by a Virginian train. *Courtesy of the Chesapeake & Ohio Historical Society*

Despite remote and rugged terrain, intrepid surveyors discovered thick seams of "smokeless" coal in the Winding Gulf region of West Virginia in the late 19th century. Equally intrepid miners starting digging the coal before the railroads could get there. The Virginian Railway arrived in 1909, coming in from the south up a tributary of the Guyandotte River. Seven years later, the Chesapeake & Ohio reached the valley, coming from the north from the New River via Beckley.

In a space of 20 miles, the two railroads used steep grades, six tunnels, an at-grade crossing, two loops, a switchback, and numerous bridges to reach the coal-rich mines. For much of the branch, they ran side-by-side and even had tracks serving the same coal tipples.

The layout focuses on the section from Pemberton, where the two railroads cross at-grade, to Stonecoal Yard. The model railroads switch four coal mines, two that are jointly served.

The Virginian tracks make a continuous loop but operate point-to-point. The majority of traffic flows from the visible staging yard past Stonecoal to the tipples on the branch and back. One or two Virginian trains per session make the run for the Woodpeck Branch located on the upper right end of the staging yard. A tipple here represents one mine, while a long yard track simulates other mines on the branch.

The layout uses a point-to-point design for the C&O. Its trains emerge from staging at Pemberton and head to the mines on the branch and/or Stonecoal Yard.

WINDING GULF — HO scale

Size: 24 x 30 feet
Prototype: C&O, Virginian
Locale: Pemberton, West Virginia
Era: 1950–1960
Style: Walk-in
Mainline run: 240 feet
Minimum radius: 30"
Turnouts: No. 6
Maximum grade: 2 percent
Train length: 20–25 hopper cars

Scale of plan: ¼" = 1 foot, 12" grid

Stonecoal Yard is the interchange point where the C&O drops off cars for the Stonecoal Branch, which is simulated by the Virginian staging yard. Although the C&O was a joint

owner of the Stonecoal Branch with the Virginian, in practice it dropped off cars here, and the Virginian delivered them to the tipples on the branch. The Virginian reaches Stonecoal Yard via a switchback at the north end at Amigo because, on the prototype, there was not room to access the yard from the south.

The turn-back loop at Winding Gulf is actually a much simplified version of the actual spaghetti bowl of track that the prototype railroads built in this valley. It omits the switchback on the C&O and a short branch on the Virginian at Loop Junction, but still replicates the feel of the entwined railroads. Upon leaving Pemberton, the C&O lines drop slightly, while the Virginian climbs so it can pass over the C&O in the peninsula. The tracks return to the same level as they approach McAlpin and Tams.

In the steam era, both railroads mostly used articulated Mallet-type 2-6-6-2 and 2-8-8-2 locomotives. In the diesel era, Virginian used 6-axle Train Masters, while the C&O relied on GP7s and GP9s. Once Norfolk Southern and CSX took over, just about any diesel from their rosters could be spotted.

Most of the old mines played out by the 1960s, but the line is still used. The CSX abandoned its tracks and shares NS tracks to access the few productive mines still in operation.

Wiscasset

This track plan attempts to capture, in scale form, the charm of the Wiscasset, Waterville & Farmington as displayed in this photo showing a portion of the restored WW&F, which is now a tourist railroad. *Joseph M. Calisi*

Wiscasset was blessed with one of the finest natural harbors on the northern New England coast. Construction of the Wiscasset, Waterville & Farmington Railway, a two-foot narrow gauge railroad, began in 1894 to bring agricultural products to the port. It reached Winslow in 1902. At the height of operation in 1921, it had 90 freight cars, 6 passenger cars and 7 engines, with a mix of Forney and Baldwin locomotives. The railroad was largely dismantled in 1934 to settle unpaid bills.

I designed this layout for a client and his new basement. The problem with the space was the constriction in width right in the middle of the long dimension. A large support pole was also an issue.

The layout features the WW&F from Wiscasset to Winslow in On30 scale. Bachmann's inexpensive, fine-running engines with DCC have made this a very popular scale. On30 trains can use HO track, but the ties are too short. Several manufacturers offer On30 track that is closer to scale and has a rustic appearance. You could also handlay track with the correct ties and spacing for a scale appearance.

While On30 allows for comparatively tight radius in curves, the O scale structures surrounding the tracks are large and need plenty of space.

The Wiscasset waterfront occupies the left corner and is the signature area of the layout, especially the long trestle across the mud flats at the town waterline. The plan dedicates a good portion of its space to depict the town of Wiscasset and waterfront scenes. The railroad wharf extends across the bump-out. Careful treatment of the backdrop is needed here.

The standard gauge Maine Central interchanged freight with the WW&F in Wiscasset. Cargo to be interchanged was manually trans-loaded from one railroad to the other. The Maine Central tracks were located slightly below the WW&F tracks so that the car floors could be on the same level.

In the layout, cars on the Maine Central are manually staged at the start of the operating session. The WW&F treats these cars as another industry to switch. It might be possible to extend the standard gauge tracks into the bump-out and make them more than just dummy tracks.

WISCASSET — On30 scale

Size: 16 x 40 feet
Prototype: Wiscasset, Waterville & Farmington
Locale: Wiscasset, Maine
Era: 1900–1930
Style: Walk-in
Mainline run: 100 feet
Minimum radius: 30"
Turnouts: No. 6
Maximum grade: 0 percent
Train length: 10 cars

Scale of plan: ¼" = 1 foot, 12" grid

The layout curves around the Maine Central crossing to approach the engine terminal in the upper yard. The upper yard was the principal maintenance facility on the WW&F. The track plan shows the arrangement that was present in 1910, so Winter's sawmill is absent.

Next, the line crosses an iron bridge to reach Weeks Mills. Weeks Mills is an important location. The plan includes a double-ended passing siding as well as a stub siding for a cannery, freight house, and station. In the prototype, a distance separated them, but the plan compresses them into one location. Instead of a wye to Albion Branch, it is represented by a staging cassette. This allows turning the trains to Albion without a space-hogging wye.

The tracks continue to the far side of the peninsula to North Vassalboro, where the large American Woolen Mills, with a stub siding to switch, is located. Several Walthers Front Street Warehouses could be kitbashed into a convincing model of this mill. The outbuildings and mill race help make this an attractive scene.

The line continues to Winslow, where a small engine terminal turns the engines and prepares them for the return trip. A wooded area and wooden trestle separates the Winslow scene from the North Vassalboro scene.

From Winslow, the plan shows an optional connection through the backdrop to create a return loop. This might be useful for an open house or test running, but would not be used in operating sessions.

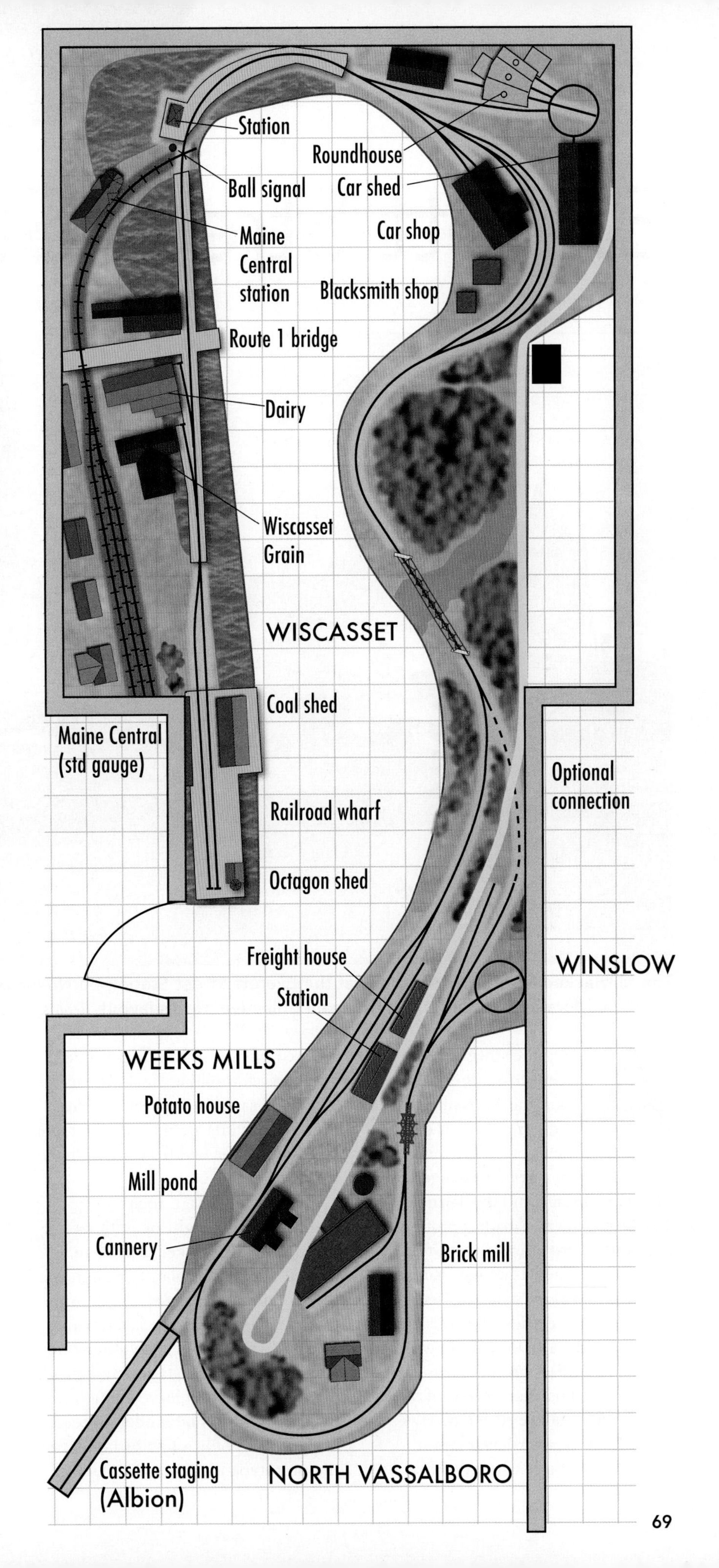

Everett Street Station

The Milwaukee Road's *Hiawatha* sits at the Everett Street Station on November 27, 1941. Re-creating a similar scene in operating model form is the main objective of this layout. *Trains Magazine collection*

Among the streamlined passenger trains of the 1930s, the Milwaukee Road's *Hiawatha* is one of the most memorable. The highly successful train carried passengers between Chicago and the Twin Cities. The beautiful train made a profit even during the hard years of the Great Depression. The Milwaukee Road used the *Hiawatha* name for several trains over the decades, but this layout focuses on the 1939–1941 era when the Milwaukee Road ran two Twin City *Hiawatha* trains, plus dozens of others, through Milwaukee each day.

Building this particular layout became a lot easier when Walthers released kits for most of the needed structures and rolling stock. In fact, you could say this inspired the idea. Some of the kits are now sold out, but they can still be had from secondhand sources.

The layout design focuses on passenger and freight operations in downtown Milwaukee. I used an official 1962 track plan to design the model railroad. Thanks to the prototype's compact size, the layout can fit in a 16 x 30 room with almost no compression in the station and freight yard areas, and still leave enough room for a workshop. The model railroad design omits only a few turnouts from the prototype arrangement. As such, it should support fully prototypical operation of the passenger and freight trains that enter the downtown area.

The Walthers' kits are slightly reduced in size compared to the prototype. For example, the station omits extensions on each end. There is room on the plan to build the full-sized station and shed, but the layout plan shows the kits in their actual size.

The curving ladders on each side of the station require some fancy handlaid track. You can take comfort in the fact the Milwaukee Road engineers faced the same challenges.

The turntable by the station, served by a three-way switch, is shown on the Sanborn maps from 1910, but it was removed before 1962. It would not have been used in operating the 1939–41 *Hiawatha*, but it would be needed if you backdate the layout to an earlier time. The station was opened in 1886, and a 19th century operating session would be fun to try.

In the prototype, the tracks on the bridge over the Menomonee Canal are straight. Due to space constraints, the model railroad has curved tracks over the bridge. You would have to make the bridge a bit wider than the prototype. Fortunately, the bridge is located in a position where that is hard to discern.

While the *Hiawatha* is the star of this layout, you should not forget the extensive freight operations that take place in the central yard. This extensive yard contains about 25 turnouts and nearly 300 feet of track. The central location of the yard allows access from both sides. The freight houses on the perimeter of the yard are modeled as reverse flats, i.e. two-dimensional models whose modeled sides face away from the aisle. You could model them in full 3-D at the expense of restricted access to the yard tracks and slightly narrower aisles.

Here, two or three operators, plus a yardmaster, will be busy switching cars during an operating session. They will be so busy spotting individual cars at the various freight houses that they will hardly notice the orange blur as the *Hiawatha* goes by.

The double-loop design creates two operational areas that are inside the loops, or the so-called "pits." To avoid having to duck under the benchwork to get to the pits, the plan includes a swing-out section by the Sixth Street Viaduct and a lift-out section at the east end of the freight yard. The lift-out section is only needed for freight trains coming from the south east. If the liftout proves problematic, it could be omitted without much loss in activity. Conversely, the track at the swing gate is vital to the operation of the layout and is not optional.

The freight and passenger trains share a common staging yard on the far wall. As is usual in most of my plans, the staging yards are visible and easily accessible.

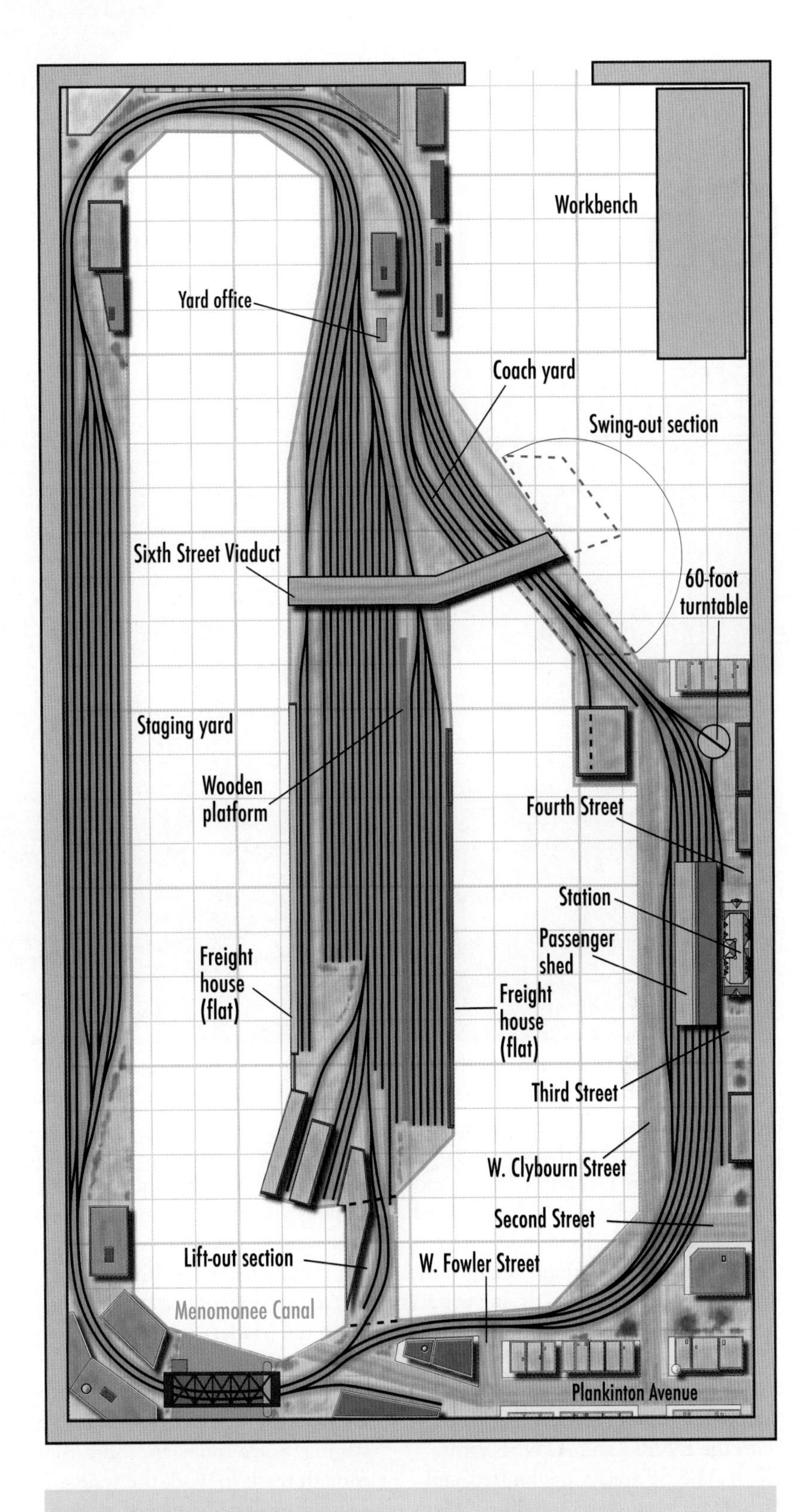

EVERETT STREET STATION — HO scale

Size: 16 x 30 feet
Prototype: Milwaukee Road
Locale: Milwaukee, Wisconsin
Era: 1939–1941
Style: Walk-in
Mainline run: 60 feet
Minimum radius: 36"
Turnouts: No. 6
Maximum grade: 0 percent
Train length: 10 passenger cars

Scale of plan: ¼" = 1 foot, 12" grid

34

Chili Line

Mixed train No. 426 crosses the Sante Fe River on December 4, 1937. Street running and the adobe church are signature elements of the Rio Grande's Chili Line. *Otto Perry, Denver Public Library collection*

An often overlooked portion of the Denver & Rio Grande is the branch that connected with the Rio Grande River on the way to Santa Fe (nicknamed the *Chili Line* because of the drying peppers hanging from roofs of area homes).

This layout models the Chili Line in a double-deck mushroom. The plan starts on the lower level at Santa Fe with the D&RG and AT&SF yards. Most AT&SF tracks are omitted, and the D&RG tracks are simplified. Many D&RG yard tracks are dual gauge, so standard gauge switching is possible.

The Rio Grande's tracks wind through the streets of town, squeezing past adobe buildings. A 2 percent grade takes the line down through the hills at Buckman and across the Rio Grande River to Espanola, New Mexico.

At Embudo, the line departs the river and climbs Barranca Hill. Helper engines assist some trains, although the newer, more powerful K-27 Mikados can usually make it without help.

At Taos Junction, a branch line splits off to the Madera Lumber Line, shown here as a simple stub staging track.

The modeled line ends at Antonito, Colorado. The small yard is visible staging. Since trains are short, there is enough track to work the trains. The engines need to be turned manually on a removable cassette as there is not room enough to model the full wye.

The 2 percent grade from Espanola and the 4 percent grade up Barranca Hill provide enough elevation change to place the upper deck of the mushroom 18" above the lower deck. The mushroom design requires constructing a raised floor in the central pit to provide the ideal viewing height. In most places, only one deck is visible at a time, avoiding a cluttered look.

Finding good running motive power and cars for HOn3 layouts is easy with Blackstone's newer models. The layout doesn't require a lot of rolling stock—a half dozen engines and a couple dozen cars is sufficient. That leaves you with lots of time to superdetail the scenery and structures.

The adobe buildings and arid scenery are a treat to model, and some commercial kits are available to speed the process.

A surprising number of trees are found on the layout, mostly cottonwoods and junipers. Since most are in the foreground, some care should be taken when making them.

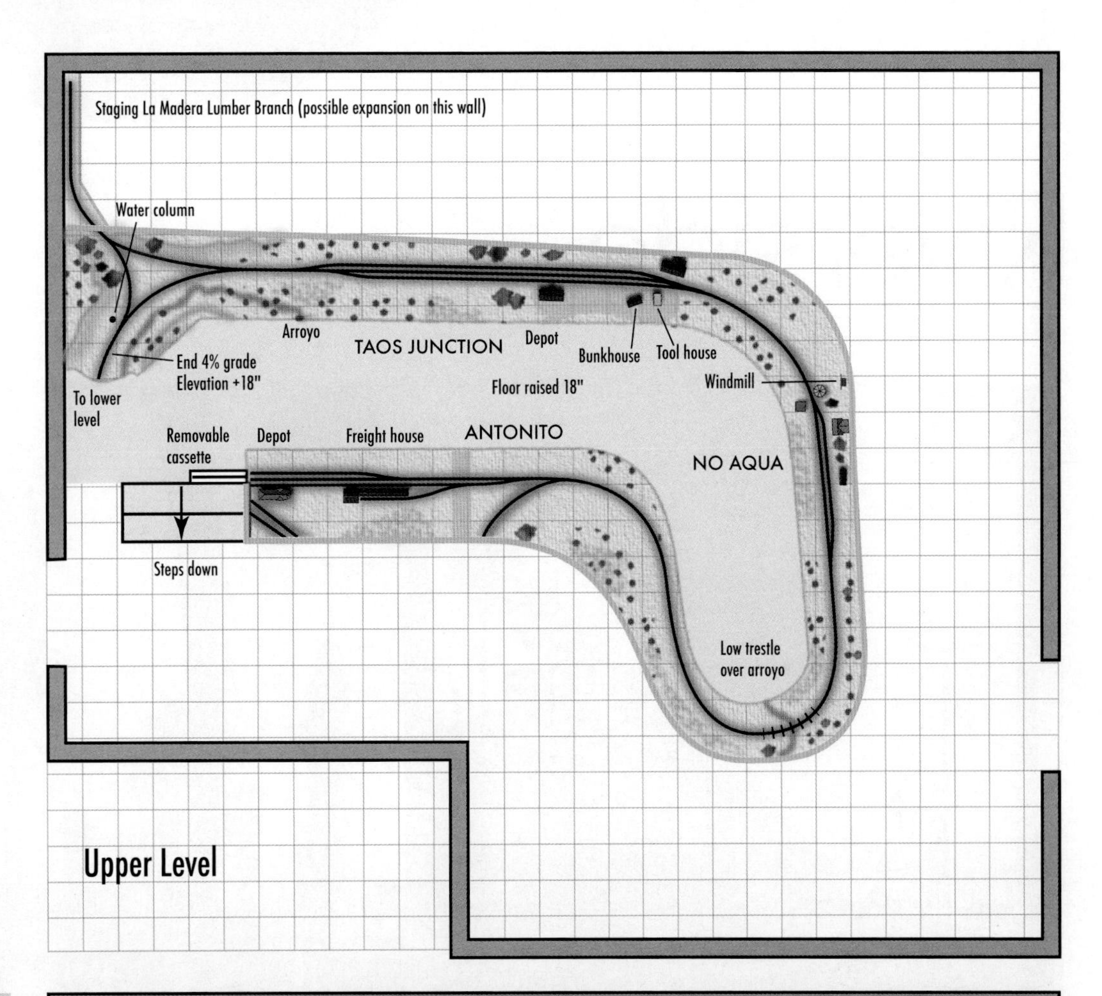

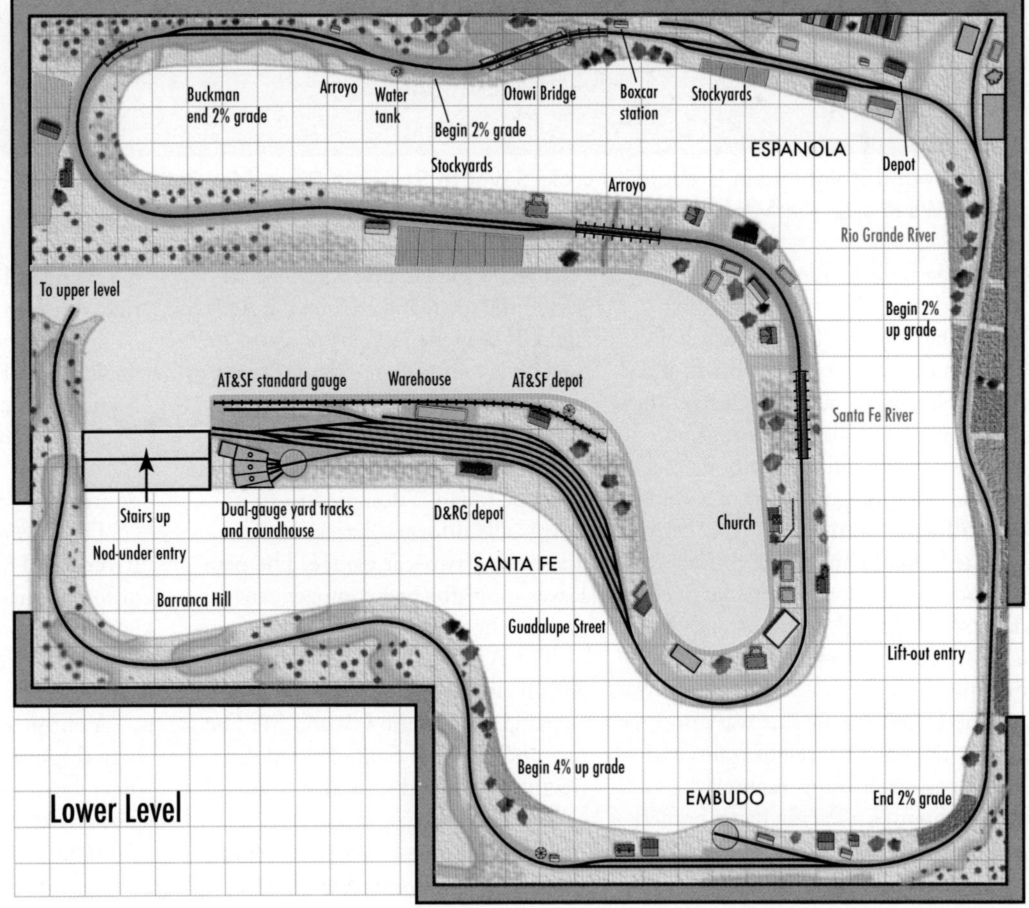

CHILI LINE — HO and HOn3 scales

Size: 24 x 30 feet
Prototype: D&RG, AT&SF
Locale: Santa Fe, New Mexico
Era: 1930–1939
Style: Walk-in, mushroom
Mainline run: 200 feet
Minimum radius: 24"
Turnouts: No. 6
Maximum grade: 4 percent
Train length: 3–10 cars

Scale of plan: 3⁄16" = 1 foot, 12" grid

35

Riverside

A westbound freight train is about to cross Seventh Street in Riverside, California, on August 3, 1946.
John L. Whitmeyer, Keith Jordan collection

Riverside, California, was a railroad hot spot in the first half of the 20th century. Four railroads served the town, and in places, they ran alongside each other. In the industrial district, dozens of businesses were rail served. Some, such as National Orange Co., were served by two different railroads.

The Santa Fe main line to Los Angeles ran through Riverside. Every day, around 18 freight trains and 2 passenger trains ran through in each direction.

The Union Pacific line was also very busy with about 10 freight trains and 4 or 5 passenger trains each way.

The Southern Pacific had a branch line that terminated here, so its traffic was lighter.

The Pacific Electric Railway also served the town and crossed the AT&SF and UP at-grade just east of town.

The layout design captures some of the action of the AT&SF, SP, and UP railroads as they pass through and/or service the industrial strip. The L-shaped plan is designed to fit in a typical California "basement," also known as a two-car garage. The plan leaves room for two compact cars to park in the garage.

The AT&SF is the primary focus, with its main line and sidetracks sandwiched between the UP and SP. The plan includes the Santa Fe depot, a freight house, and several, but not all, of its local tracks.

The SP tracks reside in the foreground of the layout. Since it is a dead-end, all trains have to be "turns" that run from and back to staging.

There is insufficient space to fully depict the UP tracks. The plan includes a small yard and some interchange tracks. You could add some additional spurs on the upper side of the L if you desire more switching action on the UP.

There were dozens of industries in Riverside. The plan includes several different businesses to add some variety, but the citrus packing houses are the main action. Some are selectively compressed to fit.

A cut in a hill and a road overpass help disguise the pair of helices that drop down to an extensive staging yard. The tracks have crossovers that allow all three railroads to share the staging tracks.

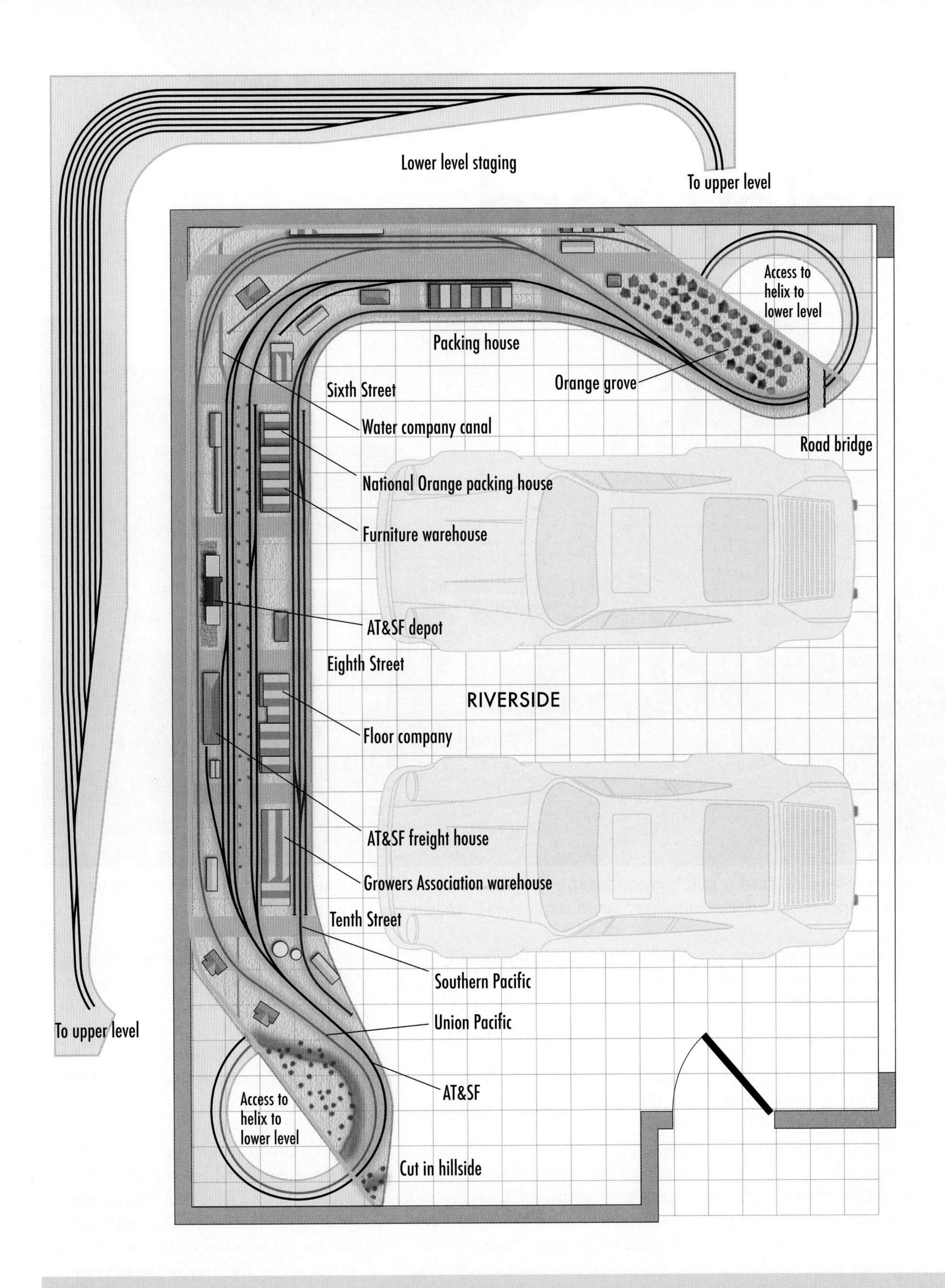

RIVERSIDE — HO scale

Size: 20 x 25 feet
Prototype: AT&SF, UP, SP
Locale: Riverside, California
Era: 1940–1949

Style: Walk-in
Mainline run: 45 feet
Minimum radius: 30"
Turnouts: No. 6

Maximum grade: 2.5 percent
Train length: 20 cars

Scale of plan: ¼" = 1 foot, 12" grid

Handley Yard

In this 1981 scene, Handley Yard is still busy, although the coal dock was out of service. In the 1950s, this yard was a busy division point yard with complete steam engine and freight car service facilities. *Rob Kitchen*

A key challenge in designing a railroad with predominantly open-top cars, like coal hoppers, is what to do with the cars when they reach staging. In most point-to-point designs, hopper cars only make one run in an operating session, and then must be manually restaged, or the loads must be removed for the return empty trip.

Another approach is to design the layout as a continuous run with a single staging yard. Hoppers that arrive in staging are then ready for a second run regardless of their load or empty status.

That is the approach this layout takes. But there is a twist: Handley, West Virginia, was in the middle of the Chesapeake & Ohio coal districts. From this division point yard, loaded coal hoppers went both east and west. While the yard did not classify coal, it sorted it by cardinal direction and sent it east to Clifton Forge, Virginia, or west to Russell, Kentucky, to be classified.

Two branches are actively modeled on the layout, Mt. Carbon and Cabin Creek. The Cabin Creek staging tracks are hidden under a mountain, but the Mt. Carbon Branch leads to the staging mole. (A *staging mole* is a term that some modelers have adopted to describe staging tracks in an out-of-the-way location where a staging operator, called *the mole*, actively stages cars.)

The mole in this layout resides in the center of the layout. The mole sorts waybills and prepares trains for the next run. Shelves below or on the back of the skyboard provide a place to store unused cars. Using a mole and double-ended staging allows a layout to run nearly continuously without the need to restage. Only the Cabin Creek Branch and the Winfrede coal load-out require manual restaging between operating sessions.

A signature scene on this layout is the Virginian crossing at Deepwater and the nearby silicon metal smelter mill at Alloy. The C&O interchanges with the Virginian on the south side of the river. The Virginian brings the cars north across the river to interchange with the New York Central.

The mill at Alloy has the largest silicon metal smelter in North America. The smelter operates around the clock, every day of the year. It produces 360,000 to 380,000 pounds of high-grade silicon metal a day, which

HANDLEY YARD — N scale

Size: 20 x 21 feet
Prototype: C&O, NYC, Virginian
Locale: Handley, West Virginia
Era: 1950–1980
Style: Walk-in
Mainline run: 150 feet
Minimum radius: 24" main line
Turnouts: No. 6
Maximum grade: 0 percent, except 4 percent Virginian connection
Train length: Fifty 50-foot coal hoppers

Scale of plan: ¼" = 1 foot, 12" grid

Mt. Carbon Branch, Elevation 48"
Virginian/NW staging
Elevation 51"
KANAWHA FALLS
End scenery
MONTGOMERY
Alkem Ferrosilicates
Virginian (NS)
Kanawha River
ALLOY
Elevation 50"
West
Barge load-out
HANDLEY
WINFREDE
THE MOLE
C&O/CSX staging
Elevation 48"
NYC (NS)
DEEPWATER
4% grade to Virginian staging
CABIN CREEK
London Locks and Dam
Power plant

represents nearly 30 percent of all industrial and commercial demand in the United States, Canada, and Mexico. One of the key inputs to the process is dirt. Coal, iron, and other materials are also needed.

The Virginian operator makes the short run out of staging, crosses the river to work cars at the mill, and interchanges with the NYC.

But the Virginian trains play a supporting role that adds some variety to the primary action on this layout—hauling coal and other goods on the C&O main line. With potentially endless mainline action, two branches, one interchange with another railroad, and a barge load-out to switch, this layout has plenty of heavy-duty railroad action.

Norfolk Southern helpers continue the Virginian's practice of shoving coal trains across the bridge at Deepwater and up the steep grades that follow. The bridge is part of a key area on the layout.

37

Montgomery

Two Burlington Junction Railway engines share the work at Sheep Yard in Montgomery in 2012. In the distance is an abandoned concrete grain elevator and an extant cement plant. *Robert Della-Pietra*

In the 1860s, the Chicago & Aurora Railroad, an ancestor to the Chicago, Burlington & Quincy, headed west from Chicago to Aurora. The line is now a BNSF main line.

Once past Aurora, the BNSF main crosses the Fox River and then splits. The BNSF Aurora Subdivision heads northwest to Minneapolis-St. Paul, while the Mendota Subdivision heads southwest to Kansas City or Denver.

Montgomery is the first control point west of Eola Yard on the Mendota Sub. In CB&Q days, the Montgomery Sheep Yard was a busy spot for livestock processing. There were 800 acres of livestock pens, feed mills, and sheep shearing stations. The sheep are long gone, but the name remained.

In 2008, the Burlington Junction Railway leased the Sheep Yard and assorted tracks from BNSF to several industries. The Burlington Junction keeps one or two engines here to service the industries, which include lumber, plastic, gravel, and steel fabricators.

A BNSF yard job out of Eola now runs cars for interchange to Sheep Yard. It drops off and picks up cars for the Burlington Junction. Then it heads to the Caterpillar plant to switch there.

While this takes place, a steady stream of mainline trains hurtles past on the Mendota Sub. These include coal, manifest freight, and an occasional intermodal train. Amtrak also uses the line.

This basement layout focuses on the industrial switching at Montgomery, but places it inside a double-track loop around the perimeter. A double-ended staging yard is in an adjoining room.

The staging should support two operators running a succession of mainline trains in each direction. Since these trains don't stop for switching, one-man crews are sufficient.

A two-man crew would take the Burlington Junction job out of Sheep Yard to work the industries. Another two-man crew could run the Eola Yard job, dropping off cars at Sheep Yard and working the Caterpillar plant before returning to staging.

To add more action, the Illinois Railway also runs here. It uses the eastern portion of the Mendota Sub to reach the former CB&Q line to Streator. It frequently waits on the connecting track in Montgomery to get clearance to head to Eola Yard, where it terminates. All in all, there is a lot of heavy rail action on this large layout.

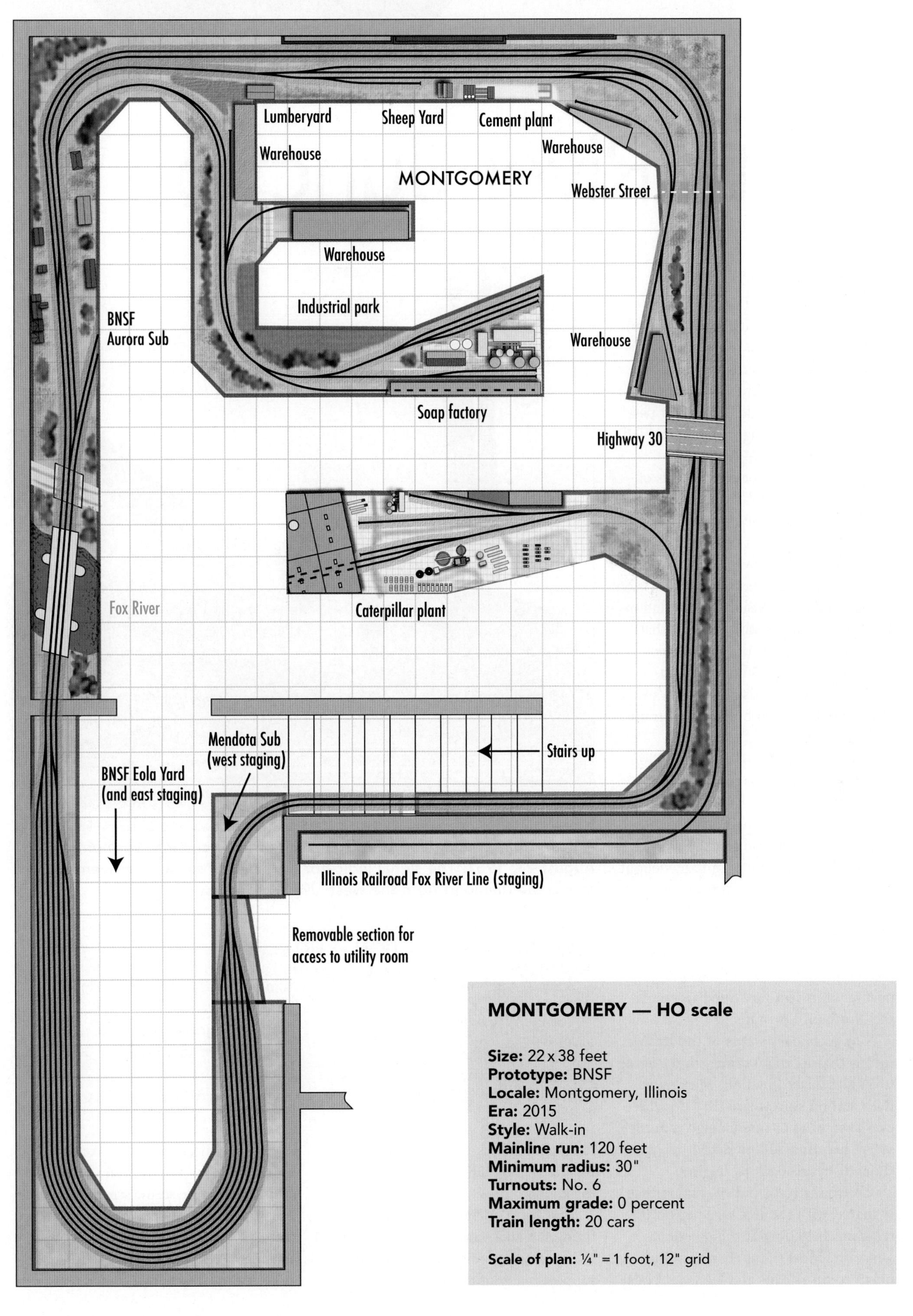

MONTGOMERY — HO scale

Size: 22 x 38 feet
Prototype: BNSF
Locale: Montgomery, Illinois
Era: 2015
Style: Walk-in
Mainline run: 120 feet
Minimum radius: 30"
Turnouts: No. 6
Maximum grade: 0 percent
Train length: 20 cars

Scale of plan: ¼" = 1 foot, 12" grid

White River Junction

The Central Vermont and Boston & Maine railroads meet at White River Junction.

The heart of the junction is the B&M diamond crossing with routes splitting from each line in three possible directions. In its heyday, dozens of passenger trains and freight trains rumbled through here every 24 hours. Most stopped to drop off or pick up cars on the four routes out of the junction.

The CV maintained an extensive freight yard northwest of town with an engine terminal, where the CV switched motive power from its Northern Division to the Southern Division. At the station area, the CV kept a yard switcher that worked its freight yard and switched passenger trains from both railroads.

The B&M was also busy at White River Junction with both freight trains and passenger trains.

The colonial revival Union Station sits alongside the diamond on a wide radius curve. A New England signature ball signal guarded the junction.

All this action and trackage makes White River Junction a railfan's delight but a layout designer's nightmare.

This track plan takes on the challenge of designing a layout for White River Junction with all four routes live. The focus is on the CV, which includes a portion of its Roxbury Subdivision of the Northern Division.

The secondary status of the B&M means that its trains come from staging to White River Junction. They make their station stop where they do whatever switching or interchange is necessary. Then they follow B&M tracks for short distances back to staging.

CV trains come out of staging that is shared with the B&M. They do the requisite switching at the junction and yard. Most trains then continue north to St. Albans and Canada. Local freight jobs work the towns of South Royalton and Randolph before heading to staging.

A staging operator can manage the trains as they come and go into staging. With active staging, the layout can support many of the area's actual trains.

The Connecticut River takes up a lot of space, but the trees and hills along its banks provide scenic screening for the return of the B&M routes radiating from White River Junction. The layout includes access hatches in the deeper sections for construction and maintenance.

A B&M train awaits departure from White River Junction, Vermont, on August 27, 1951. The signal indicator (one ball) is set for a movement across the diamond from the west. *Jim Shaughnessy*

WHITE RIVER JUNCTION — HO scale

Size: 22 x 38 feet
Prototype: CV, B&M
Locale: White River Junction, Vermont
Era: 1950–1959
Style: Walk-in
Mainline run: 220 feet
Minimum radius: 30" main line
Turnouts: No. 6
Maximum grade: 0 percent
Train length: 15–20 cars

Scale of plan: ¼" = 1 foot, 12" grid

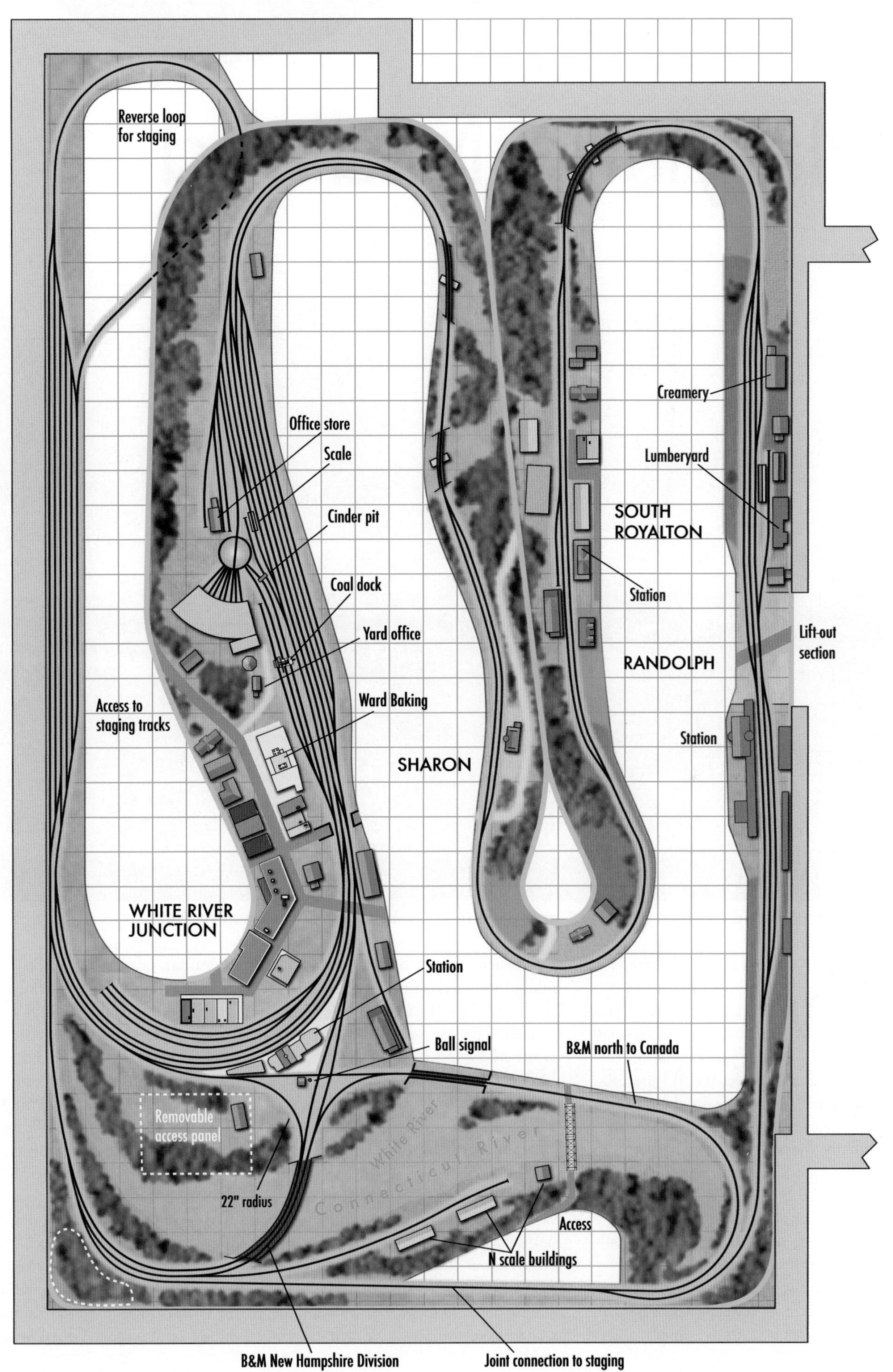

Reverse loop for staging
Office store
Scale
Cinder pit
Coal dock
Yard office
Ward Baking
Access to staging tracks
SHARON
WHITE RIVER JUNCTION
Station
Ball signal
Removable access panel
22" radius
White River
Connecticut River
Access
N scale buildings
B&M New Hampshire Division
Joint connection to staging
B&M north to Canada
Creamery
Lumberyard
SOUTH ROYALTON
Station
RANDOLPH
Lift-out section
Station

39

Maryland Midland

Maryland Midland GP38-2s work hard up the grade at Sabillasville curve in August 2005.

When I proposed the oNetrak concept to Northern Virginia Ntrak at an annual Christmas party, the idea was hotly received, literally, as the poster board I used to illustrate the idea was accidentally set afire by one of the holiday candles. Luckily, the host of the party was a professional firefighter, and he quickly doused the flames, but the oNetrak idea was launched. Later, the club developed a set of oNetrak modules depicting the Chesapeake & Ohio Mountain Subdivision.

The oNetrak concept works best when it is set up with a unified theme such as the C&O Mountain Subdivision or the Florida East Coast Modelers oNetrak layout. The layouts depicted here use a unified theme based on the Maryland Midland Railway.

The Maryland Midland is a short line that grew out of the abandoned Western Maryland Tide Subdivision. The main yard at Union Bridge hosts the largest customer on the line, Lehigh Cement. The cement plant was reached via tracks running down Farquhar Street. (Those were recently removed, but they were in operation in 2005 when this layout is set.)

The horseshoe curve at Sabillasville at the top of the Owens Creek canyon is a railfan favorite. The Maryland Midland interchanges with CSX at Highfield and Emory Grove.

The smaller layout depicts two towns, Union Bridge and Thurmont. These modules are fairly conventional rectangles except that they are built in 5-foot increments because 5 feet makes more efficient use of 8-foot lumber when cutting the frame members, and they are not much harder to transport than 4-foot-long modules. Two end-turn modules create a loop.

In the larger layout, a set of specialized modules focuses on Sabillasville, the twin bridges in Owens Creek canyon, and Emory Grove, which

WHAT IS ONETRAK?
oNetrak is a modular standard compatible with Ntrak but utilizing only one main line instead of three. The minimum module size is 1 x 4, but people have built smaller and much larger modules as well. By only requiring one line, oNetrak modules can be used to re-create almost any prototype location.

MARYLAND MIDLAND — N scale

Size: 23 x 17 feet
Prototype: Maryland Midland
Locale: Union Bridge, Maryland
Era: 2005
Style: Modular
Mainline run: 50 feet
Minimum radius: 18"
Turnouts: No. 6
Maximum grade: 0 percent
Train length: 20–30 cars

Scale of plan: ¼" = 1 foot, 12" grid

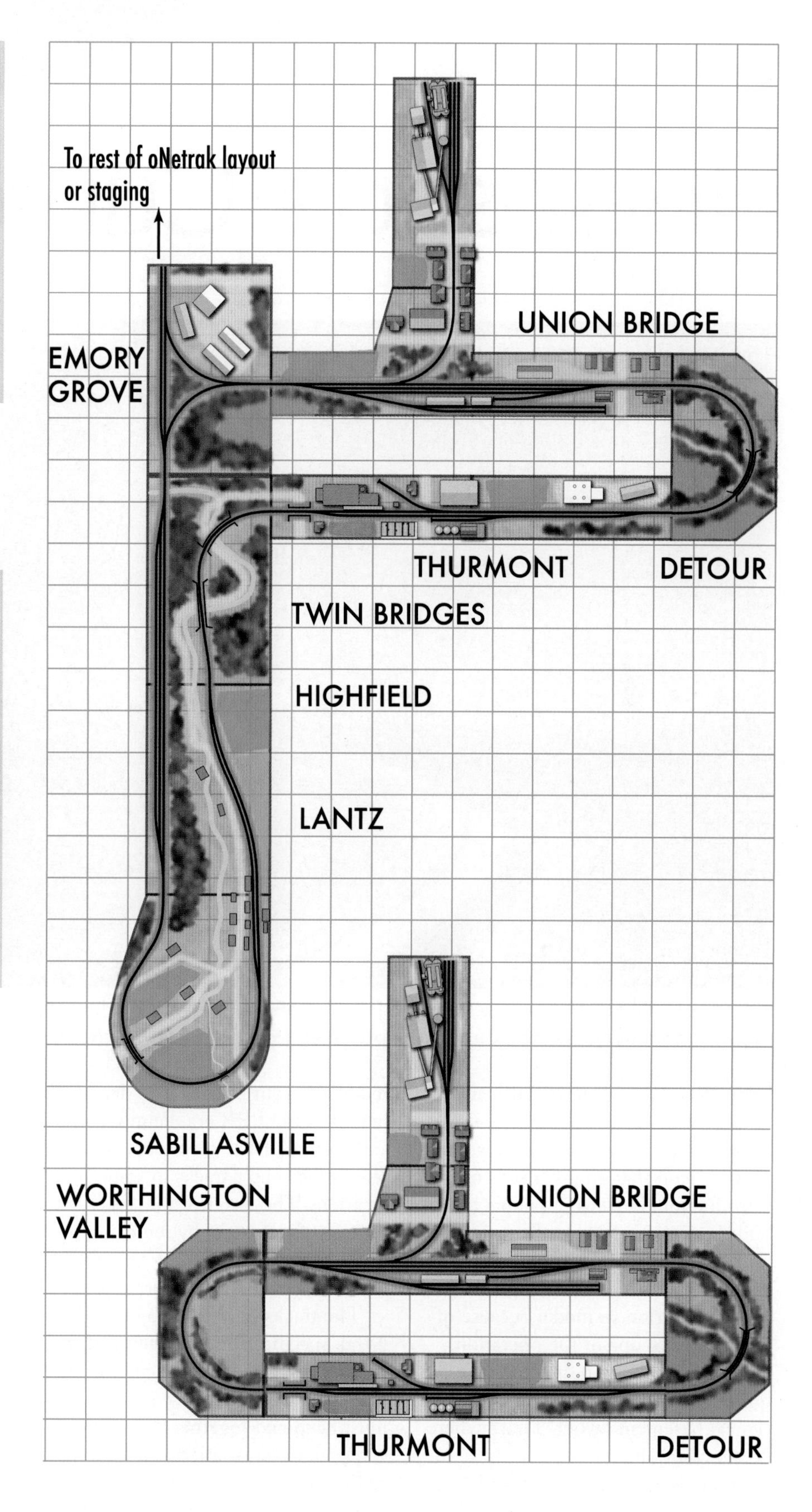

replaces the Worthington Valley end-turn module. Emory Grove is a oNetrak wye module that allows loop, point-to-point, or "red-line" running (i.e. continuous running) in a larger show. This layout has four sidings for meets. Highfield could also be used as a staging yard. Alternatively, a separate staging yard could be located at the upper left at Emory Grove.

As these designs show, modular layouts offer a lot of flexibility in setup and operation. The modules themselves need not be simple rectangles. Other shapes are possible and encouraged if they can fit in the rectangular grid at their interfaces.

Horseshoe Curve

An uneasy alliance between a Pennsy J1 2-10-4 and a Baldwin Sharknose leads a train of Pacific Fruit Express reefers uphill at Horseshoe Curve in September 1953. *Thomas J. McNamara*

The Pennsylvania Railroad's Horseshoe Curve in central Pennsylvania is a railroad icon that almost needs no introduction. Dozens of people have built layouts in all scales featuring this famous climb from Altoona up the slope of the Alleghenies. But it is not an easy location to model because of the massive scope of the operation. The four-track main line and wide horseshoe curve are difficult to fit in a typical basement layout. That's where Ntrak comes in.

Ntrak is a standard for N scale modules that is followed worldwide. The standard calls for a three-track main line and broad 24" minimum radius curves. There is an optional standard for a fourth track, and this modular layout utilizes it to depict the height of the PRR era. Penn Central and Conrail, PRR successors, removed one of the center tracks in some locations. The layout would be easy to redesign for that era by removing one of the mains and minding the spacing in between the Ntrak interfaces.

The tracks only have to meet the Ntrak specification for spacing at their extremities. The track spacing inside dedicated sections (those sections that must be joined together in a certain way) can have variations in the track spacing to match the prototype scene. The dedicated sections in this design are indicated by dotted lines between the sections in the layout diagram.

Groups that combine modules from several people under a unified theme are subsets of the Ntrak community that can have spectacular results. Ntrak participants tend to call modular sets like this a "subdivision." The Columbia River Ntrak and the C&O New River Subdivision groups did this with remarkable success. Fitting a large Ntrak subdivision into an Ntrak layout can be more difficult than fitting a set of standard 4-foot modules, but the results are usually worth it.

In this design, each module is limited to a maximum of 3 x 5 feet. Experience shows that modules larger than this are hard to move, especially if they also have a lot of vertical terrain. Thus, some of the major features, like the curve, are spread across three or four modules.

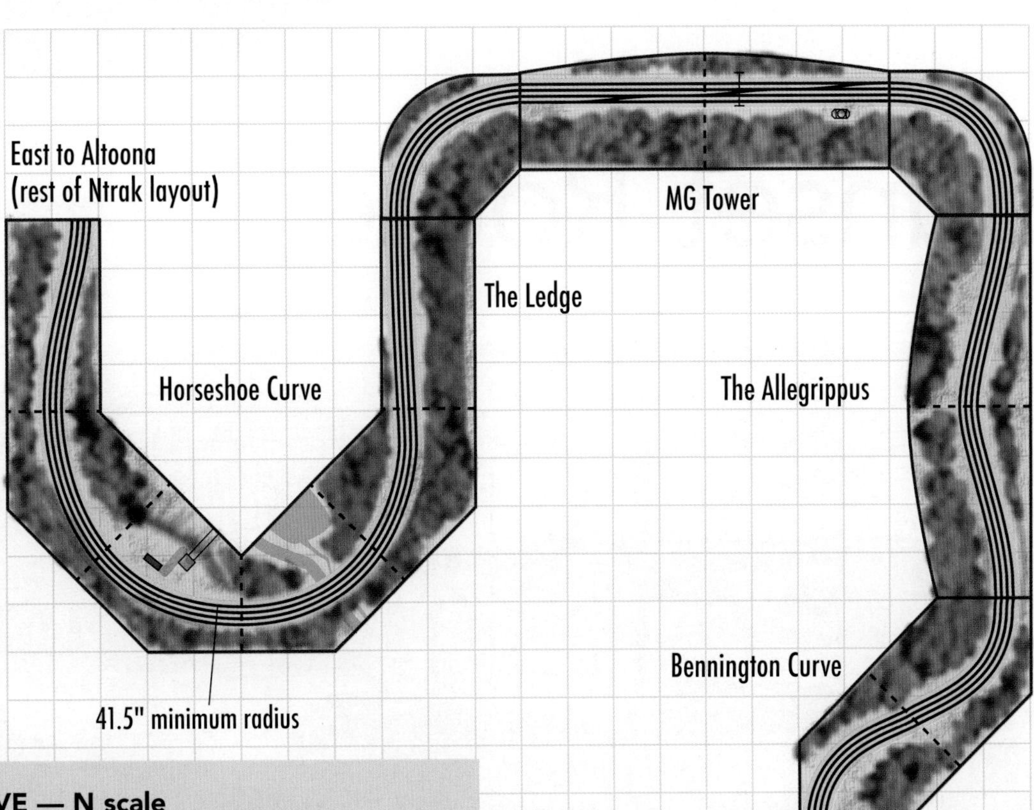

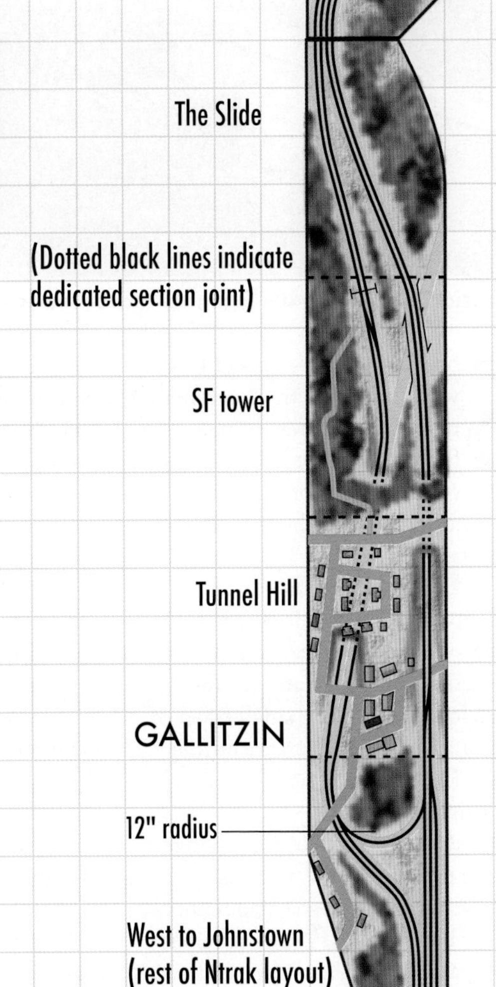

HORSESHOE CURVE — N scale

Size: 22 x 38 feet
Prototype: Pennsylvania Railroad
Locale: Gallitzin, Pennsylvania
Era: 1950–1960
Style: Modular
Mainline run: 60 feet
Minimum radius: 24" on main line, 12" at Gallitzin Loop
Turnouts: No. 8
Maximum grade: 0 percent
Train length: 100 cars

Scale of plan: ¼" = 1 foot, 12" grid

Even with the large size of the layout, the design includes some selective compression. The 12" radius loop curve at Gallitzin is especially tight and could cause problems for large steamers that try to negotiate it, but this tight radius is needed if the module width is kept under 3 feet.

The radius at the curve is generous for N scale at 41.5", a scale 553 feet. Even at this size, it is still tighter than the 600-foot radius of the prototype curve.

Ntrak layouts do not generally allow grades, so this layout is built flat. But in some circumstances, the layout could be installed with a grade using spacers under the legs, as long as room for the return to base level is provided by the rest of the layout.

41

Sunset Route

A classic D&RGW SD40T-2 tunnel motor leads a piggyback train across the Colorado River into Yuma in 1998.

Southern Pacific's Sunset Route was the second transcontinental railroad across the United States. After the Union Pacific takeover of SP, traffic on the route grew, and today, it is a busy route with 40–50 trains a day.

The Gila Subdivision runs from Yuma to Tucson. This layout focuses on the sub's western end, which loops east from Yuma around the Gila Mountains to the small town of Welton and the junction with the former Phoenix Sub, now just an industrial track.

All trains stop at Yuma to change crews. The majority of traffic is intermodal, either double-stack containers or piggyback trailers. While manifest freight, automobile, and chemical trains also run, there are few coal trains on the line.

The focus of this HO scale layout is on running long trains. The sidings can handle 30-car trains with three units on the head end. Most of the trains run through, but the yard does some classification for westbound trains, and a switch job works the Yuma sidings.

The plan includes signature elements such as twin bridges over the Colorado River, irrigated farm fields, canals, a mission, and the Territorial Prison.

The inside of the J-shaped peninsula depicts the area where the railroad skirts the edge of the Gila Mountains. The railroad maintains a steady grade as it snakes across the foothills. This area includes horseshoe curves, cuts, and fills.

The layout's route is mostly double-tracked, with two sections of single track. The long single-track run from East Yard to Kinter is the main operational bottleneck.

SUNSET ROUTE — HO scale

Size: 22 x 50 feet
Prototype: UP Gila Sub
Locale: Yuma, Arizona
Era: 2004–2010
Style: Walk-in
Mainline run: 300 feet
Minimum radius: 30" on main line
Turnouts: No. 8
Maximum grade: 0 percent
Train length: 30 cars

Scale of plan: 3⁄8" = 1 foot, 12" grid

The line is CTC controlled, which requires a dispatcher, who can be located under the stairs, to operate a control panel. However, adding an operational signal system may not be an easy task.

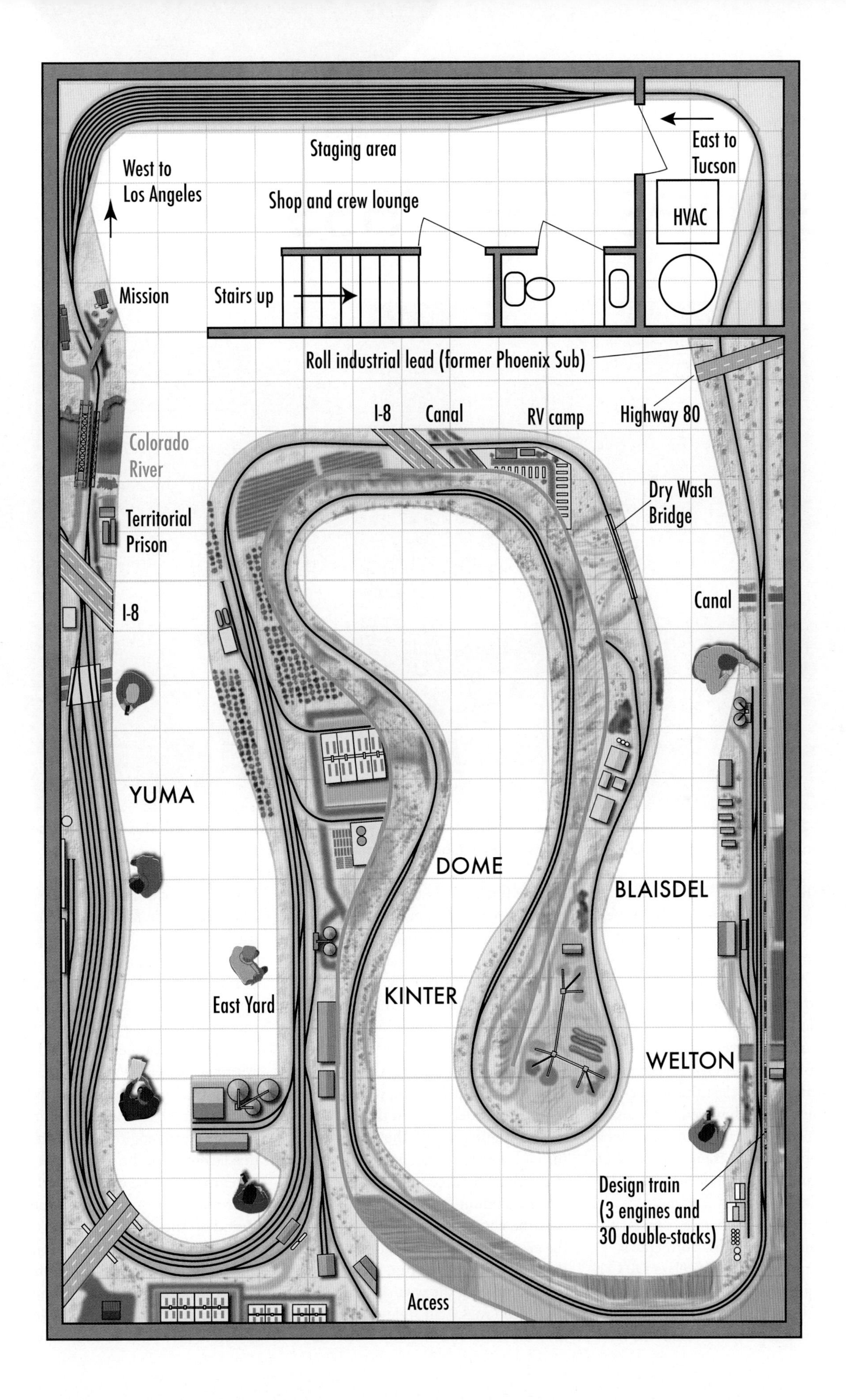
Staging area
West to
Los Angeles
East to
Tucson
Shop and crew lounge
HVAC
Mission
Stairs up
Roll industrial lead (former Phoenix Sub)
I-8
Canal
RV camp
Highway 80
Colorado
River
Dry Wash
Bridge
Territorial
Prison
I-8
Canal
YUMA
DOME
BLAISDEL
KINTER
East Yard
WELTON
Design train
(3 engines and
30 double-stacks)
Access

42

Tennessee Pass

A 2-8-8-2 Mallet, D&RGW no. 3602, pulls a westbound freight with 70 cars under the telltales of Tennessee Pass Tunnel in September 1931. *Otto Perry, Denver Public Library collection*

The Denver & Rio Grande Western Tennessee Pass Line, at 10,212 feet, is the highest main line in the United States, and it is also one of the steepest. During WWII, traffic boomed, and this is the time period depicted in the track plan.

Minturn is a crew change point and site of the helper engine terminal. Little switching or classification occurs in Minturn Yard. However, the Malta Turn is made up in the yard from blocks dropped by manifest trains for switching in town and the few industries on the line. Malta is modeled in staging.

Helpers with a separate crew tack on the end of the train. Both crews throttle up the grade. Wireless DCC is a key requirement for this operation.

Upon leaving the yard, the tracks pass Rex, where a 2 percent grade kicks in.

The track enters the steep Eagle River Canyon and approaches Belden. The plan depicts both sides of the canyon since the railroad built the siding across the creek from the main. The Gilman Mine tipple is in the canyon.

After passing the mining town of Red Cliff, the tracks reach Pando. Here, Camp Hale, home of the U.S. Army 10th Mountain Division, was located. The camp is depicted on the backdrop.

Continuing uphill, the tracks punch through Deen Tunnel and then traverse the famous S curves at Mitchell.

The summit tunnel at 62.4" elevation caps the climb. Tennessee Pass siding on the east end is a key location and marks the end of the visible run. Here, helpers cut and turn on the wye.

A deep rocky cut hides the entrance into the helix and staging. The helix has three tracks and four turns at 2 percent grade for nearly 650 feet of track. Trains can be staged in a serial or head-to-toe manner. There is plenty of room inside the helix for a staging operator to manage the trains and get them ready for their next run.

This is an all-steam railroad. Although D&RGW had some diesels during this time period, they did not run on Tennessee Pass. Amassing the O scale steam engines needed for this layout could be a challenge and potentially expensive. In the interest of economy, you could move the time period on the layout up to the transition era, without too much anachronistic drama, except that the second bore of the Tennessee Pass Tunnel would be missing. Traffic would also be less, and Camp Hale would be shut down.

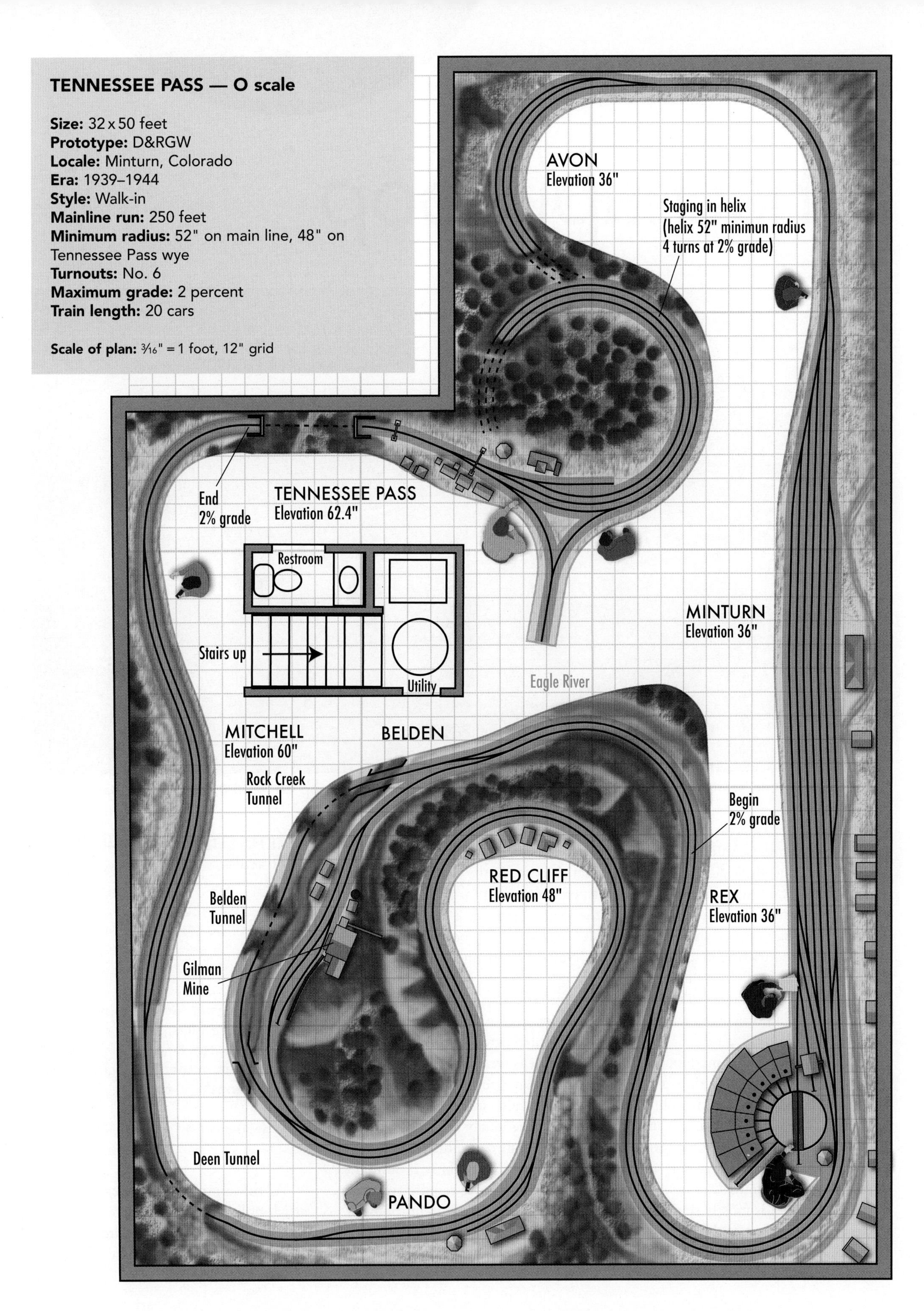

TENNESSEE PASS — O scale
Size: 32 x 50 feet
Prototype: D&RGW
Locale: Minturn, Colorado
Era: 1939–1944
Style: Walk-in
Mainline run: 250 feet
Minimum radius: 52" on main line, 48" on Tennessee Pass wye
Turnouts: No. 6
Maximum grade: 2 percent
Train length: 20 cars
Scale of plan: 3⁄16" = 1 foot, 12" grid
AVON
Elevation 36"
Staging in helix
(helix 52" minimun radius
4 turns at 2% grade)
End
2% grade
TENNESSEE PASS
Elevation 62.4"
Restroom
Stairs up
Utility
MINTURN
Elevation 36"
Eagle River
MITCHELL
Elevation 60"
BELDEN
Rock Creek
Tunnel
Begin
2% grade
RED CLIFF
Elevation 48"
REX
Elevation 36"
Belden
Tunnel
Gilman
Mine
Deen Tunnel
PANDO

43

Tehachapi Loop

Amid spring-green scenery, a BNSF intermodal train grinds up Tehachapi Loop on April 1, 2010. *Mike Danneman*

Tehachapi Loop is one of the most famous American railroad locations. Built during 1875–76 by the Southern Pacific, the line became part of the Union Pacific in 1996, when it absorbed the SP. BNSF trains also use the loop under trackage rights. The line features heavy traffic over its steep grade and twisty climb though California's semiarid Tehachapi Mountains.

Focus of this layout is modern train running. Multiple decks produce a 400-foot-long (336 visible) main line arrayed in a loop-to-loop plan. Even with 10 scale miles of run, some features such as Cliff, Bealville siding, and some tunnels had to be omitted.

The track plan is mostly single track. However, some of the smaller sidings have been combined into sections of double track.

On the layout, the prototype's 2 percent grade would climb too high over the run, so the grade is just under 1 percent (except for the region near the loop where it is 2 percent to allow clearance over the loop tunnel).

Normal traffic includes intermodal, oil tank cars, auto racks, and manifest freights. The staging scheme uses yards at the top level and on the lowest level, which is dedicated just to staging. Both staging areas terminate in loops. Since there are few open-top loads on the line, most trains can traverse the loops and be immediately ready for a second run on the railroad. This also allows trains to run continuously if desired.

Several industries require switching, enough to keep a local freight busy. Edison is active with half a dozen packing houses, and the Arvin Branch could require a second local switch job.

TEHACHAPI LOOP — N scale

Size: 22 x 38 feet
Prototype: BNSF, UP
Locale: Tehachapi, California
Era: 2015
Style: Walk-in
Mainline run: 336 feet (visible)
Minimum radius: 18"
Turnouts: No. 8
Maximum grade: 2 percent
Train length: 50 cars

Scale of plan: 3⁄16" = 1 foot, 12" grid

At the summit, the cement plant at Monolith is a major switch job. A food products industry located on the outskirts of Tehachapi also ships tank cars.

Upper Level

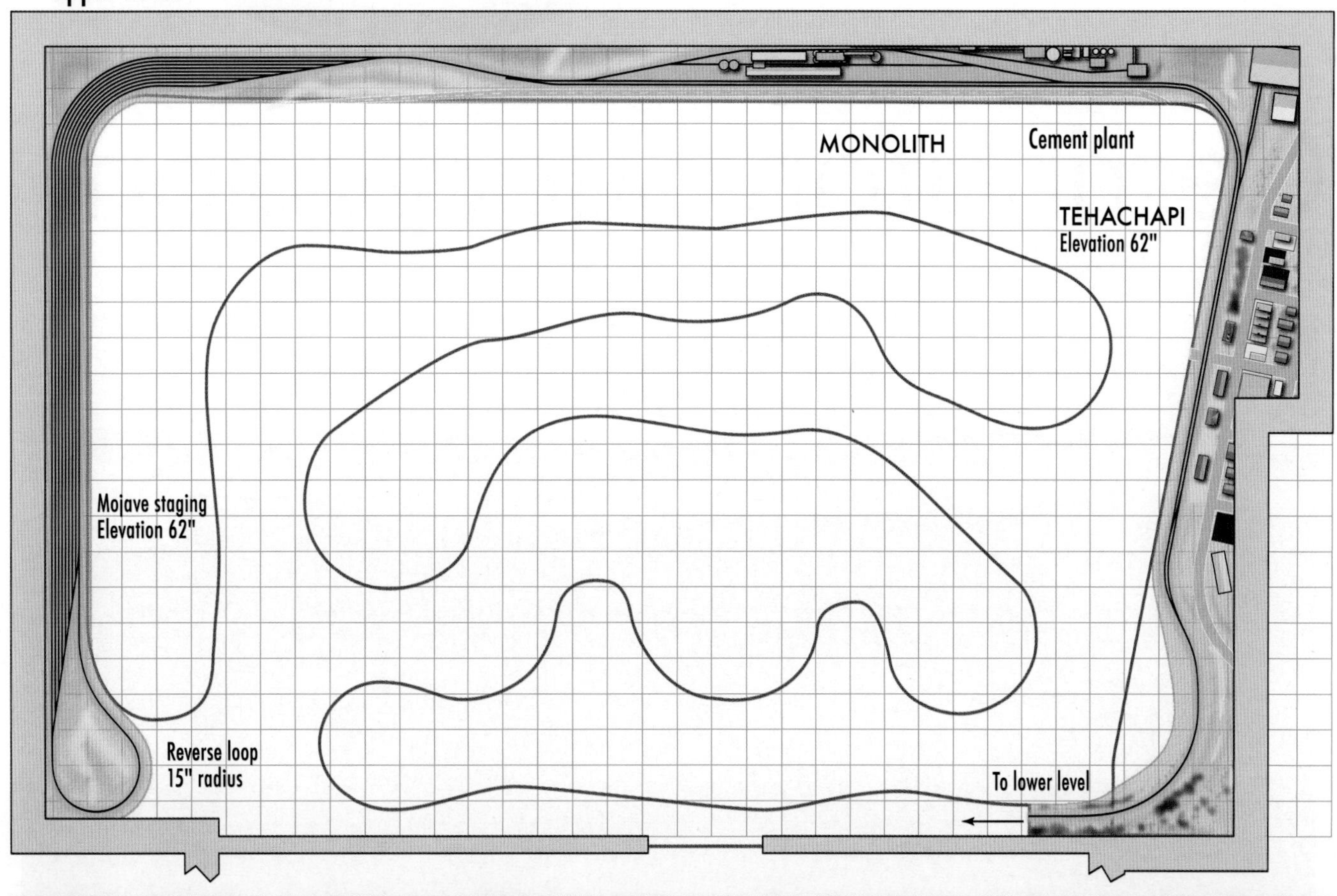

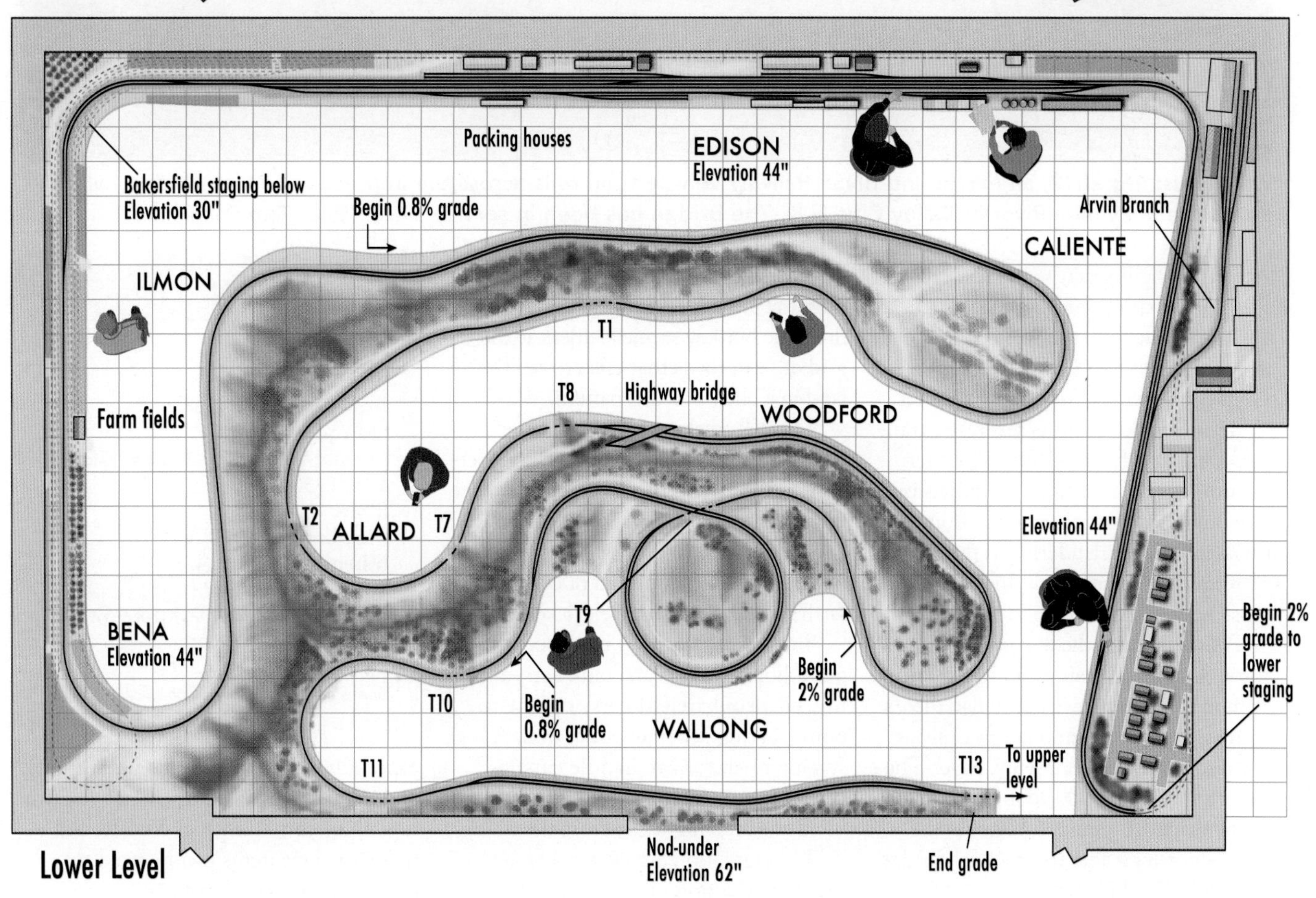

Lower Level

44

Carrington Subdivision

On August 18, 2012, an eastbound BNSF Railway vehicle train rolls across the impressive Hi-Line Bridge, which spans the Sheyenne River at Valley City, N.D. The bridge has been in service since 1908. *Tom Danneman*

Angling across the sparsely settled farmland of North Dakota, the western half of the Soo Line's Minnesota Division is one of Soo's busiest routes.

This S scale layout is set in the transition era and focuses on the southern portion of the Carrington Subdivision. The modeled portion extends from the division point at Enderlin to the town of Rogers, where there is an a diamond crossing with the Northern Pacific.

Along the way, the line passes through miles of prairie and wheat farms. Although the profile is pretty flat, there's plenty of great topography, especially as the line follows the Sheyenne River. The watercourse cuts a 200-foot-deep coulee in the plains. A scenic highlight is the 3,860-foot-long and 160-foot-tall bridge at Valley City. This works out to 2.5 feet in scale, so some selection compression might be necessary. Another less dramatic but key scenic element is the grid of farm roads that crisscrosses the land in a checkerboard pattern.

The NP tracks at the crossing at Rogers extend into staging. During operating sessions, this can be treated as a live interchange. That is, a short NP train can back onto the layout to pick up and set out cars at Rogers. Instead of continuing farther south, it heads back to staging.

Since most traffic is in closed-top grain hoppers, boxcars, tank cars, and miscellaneous freight cars, a point-to-point staging scheme works well. A staging operator can handle cars in between runs by flipping waybills and hand transferring cars across the aisle.

The transition era currently has the best selection of S scale products, especially supporting items like vehicles and details. There is also an active farm modeling community in S scale, and many of their items can be used to detail this granger layout.

CARRINGTON SUBDIVISION — S scale

Size: 46 x 68 feet
Prototype: Soo Line, Northern Pacific
Locale: Valley City, North Dakota
Era: 1950–1955
Style: Walk-in
Mainline run: 370 feet
Minimum radius: 42"
Turnouts: No. 6
Maximum grade: 0.5 percent
Train length: 26 cars

Scale of plan: ⅛" = 1 foot, 24" grid

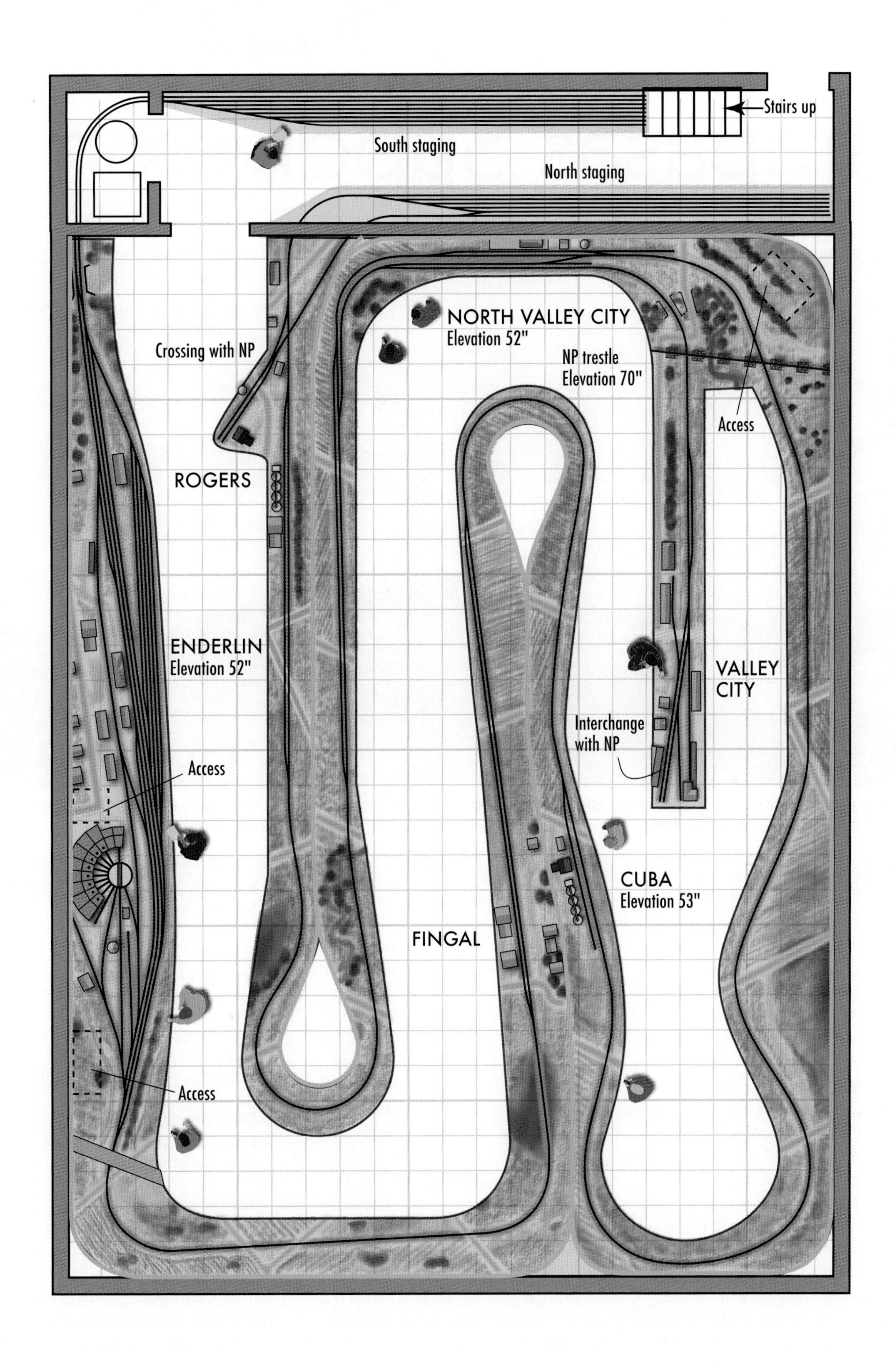
Stairs up
South staging
North staging
NORTH VALLEY CITY
Elevation 52"
Crossing with NP
NP trestle
Elevation 70"
Access
ROGERS
ENDERLIN
Elevation 52"
VALLEY
CITY
Interchange
with NP
Access
CUBA
Elevation 53"
FINGAL
Access

45

Lampasas Subdivision

A Santa Fe GP7u, no. 2015, leads two BN geeps on the local job as it switches the grain elevator just south of Temple, Texas, in September 1998. The distinctive Santa Fe searchlight signals were still in service at this time.

In 1995, the Atchison, Topeka & Santa Fe merged with the Burlington Northern. As a result, the former AT&SF lines through Temple, Texas, became much busier, with 40–50 trains a day. About half head west from Temple on the Lampasas Subdivision. The trains on the Lampasas Sub are a varied lot with unit coal trains, intermodals, manifest freights, local freights, trackage-right trains from short lines, and solid military trains.

On the edge of hill country, the region features ridges, arroyos, and other obstacles the railroad has to snake around. The subdivision's east end is suburban. Past Fort Hood, the area becomes more rural with farms and forests of scrub live oaks, junipers, and cottonwoods. The simple scenery is well suited to a layout with narrow benchwork.

The design challenge was accommodating the long yard at Temple and the traffic flowing through it. Half the trains passing through Temple Yard do not take the Lampasas Sub. To simulate this traffic, one large staging yard represents both Fort Worth to the north and Houston-Galveston to the south. Some trains leave staging, go through Temple Yard, and then head back to staging on tracks parallel to the ones they just took to enter the yard.

Once on the modeled part of the subdivision, Lampasas Sub trains traverse about 500 feet of main line with four passing sidings, and interact with the Gulf, Colorado & San Saba, Fort Worth & Western, and U.S. Army Railroad at Fort Hood. Fort Hood is a busy location that requires a separate operating position to switch the railhead.

LAMPASAS SUBDIVISION — HO scale

Size: 52 x 70 feet
Prototype: BNSF
Locale: Temple, Texas
Era: 1996–2001
Style: Walk-in
Mainline run: 600 feet
Minimum radius: 42" main line, 36" branch line
Turnouts: No. 6
Maximum grade: 0 percent
Train length: 30 cars

Scale of plan: ⅛" = 1 foot, 24" grid

The line is fully signaled with sections of Centralized Traffic Control near Temple and Brownwood and Absolute Permissive Block signals elsewhere.

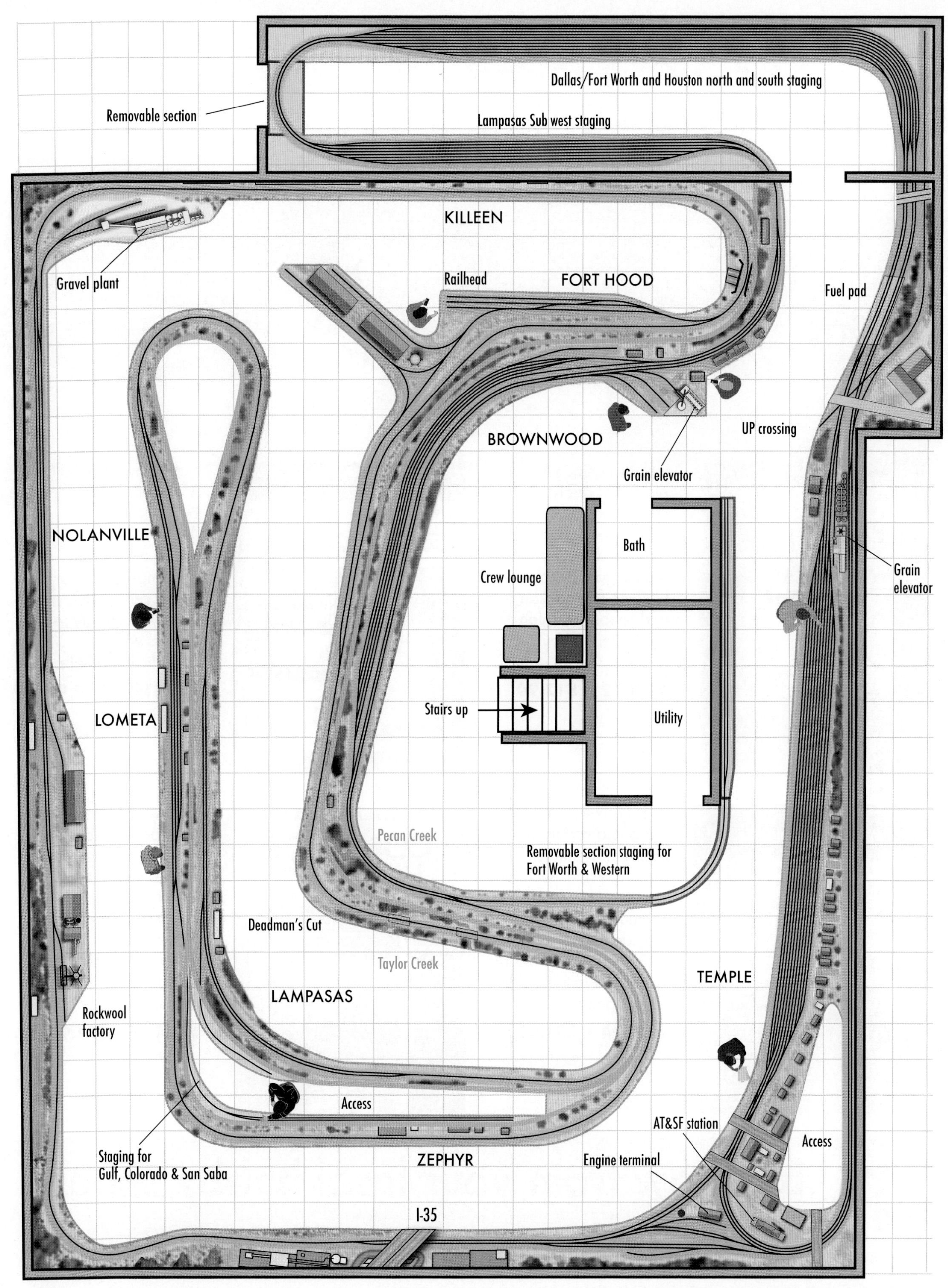

Dallas/Fort Worth and Houston north and south staging
Removable section
Lampasas Sub west staging
KILLEEN
Gravel plant
Railhead
FORT HOOD
Fuel pad
UP crossing
BROWNWOOD
Grain elevator
NOLANVILLE
Bath
Crew lounge
Grain elevator
LOMETA
Stairs up
Utility
Pecan Creek
Removable section staging for
Fort Worth & Western
Deadman's Cut
Taylor Creek
TEMPLE
LAMPASAS
Rockwool
factory
Access
AT&SF station
Access
Staging for
Gulf, Colorado & San Saba
ZEPHYR
Engine terminal
I-35